Making Charities Effective

A Guide for Charities and Voluntary Bodies

Making Charities Effective

A Guide for Charities and Voluntary Bodies

Peter L. George FCIB

Foreword by The Rt. Hon. Michael Alison MP

Jessica Kingsley Publishers
London

First published in 1989 by
Jessica Kingsley Publishers
13 Brunswick Centre
London WC1N 1AF

British Library Cataloguing in Publication Data

George, Peter L.
  Making charities effective: a guide for charities and voluntary bodies.
  1. England. Charities. Administration - Manuals
  I. Title.
  361.7'632'0942

ISBN 1-83502-023-0
ISBN 1-85302-019-2 Pbk
Printed in Great Britain by
Billing & Sons Ltd, Worcester

To my wife, Margaret, the best encourager
and without whom this could never have been written.

Note: Throughout the book the expression 'he' should be taken to include 'she'.

Contents

List of Figures

Foreword

It is a privilege to be allowed to contribute a foreword to a book which is destined to become a standard and enduring work of reference in a field of the utmost significance.

It is difficult to over-state the value and significance of voluntary and charitable bodies in a free society. They are at once symptoms and causes. Symptoms, because they could neither exist nor flourish in authoritarian or totalitarian societies. Active and effective voluntary organisations depend upon a differentiated social structure in which the economic system, the political system, and the moral-cultural system are free, complementary and not subordinate to over-riding state control. Where voluntary bodies abound and flourish, there you may discern and indeed define a free society.

But such bodies are more than symptoms. They actually cause, and help to create, free societies. Charitable and voluntary organisations - from giant private business corporations, through the various churches, to the most modest welfare group or association - represent what Professor Michael Novak has described as 'mediating structures': groupings of men and women transcending the individual, but smaller than the state, in which human initiative, co-operation, and accountability can flourish. They represent a defence, a security against the power of the state; indeed they form the environment in which state accountability may itself be properly registered and maintained.

Charitable and voluntary bodies abound in Britain, like numberless stars in the firmament of our freedom. At the end of 1986 there were over 158,000 separate charities on the register of the Charity

Commission for England and Wales alone and the number was growing at the rate of 4,000 a year. According to the Charities Aid Foundation, these charities had an annual income of £12.7 *billion* in 1985/86:
they covered a dazzling, bewildering multiplicity of causes in the fields
of medicine and health; international aid of various kinds; general welfare, such as child care; animal protection; religious and missionary
work; heritage and the environment; youth work; and the arts. The
common denominator was to be found in Peter George's luminous
broad-brush definition of a charity, i.e., an 'organisation which is working to benefit others in the interests of the good of society and in which
the members of the top supervisory body normally receive no personal
benefit.'

I have been at pains to stress the unique value and significance of
voluntary and charitable bodies as the very cells and corpuscles of the
good society. How vital it is that such cells should be sound and healthy.
How indispensable, therefore, is this book of reference, guidance, and
definition which Peter George has drafted: the basic 'medical' text
book for checking and maintaining the health of charitable bodies.
How astonishing, indeed, that we should have had to wait so long before this work appeared: how could we have managed without it? And
how miraculous that a retired banker and manager, a devotee and dis-
ciple of figures, should have proved capable of such easy flowing, lite-
rate prose! The world of charities, but indirectly a much wider world
too, will long remain in Peter George's debt.

The Rt Hon Michael Alison, MP
23rd March 1989

Introduction

Over the last three years various friends have asked me to help them with problems they were experiencing in their charities. It became obvious that in each case there was confusion in the minds of some, if not all, of those involved about the role and responsibilities of trustees, and their relationship to the full time member of staff whom I shall refer to as the 'executive officer'. Both smaller charities and charities employing many staff seem to be equally affected.

As long as these principles were unclear each issue seemed a huge problem in itself, unrelated to other problems. Once the principles on which such organisations operate were clarified, however, the particular circumstances of each case could be looked at and a way forward found.

In 1986 I was asked by an international Christian charity to travel to Kenya to conduct some workshops on the subject of how to help their national boards of trustees become more effective. I found that discussion of these matters in a workshop environment was a fruitful way to help those involved unravel some of the principles and talk through their very different problems. It also showed me the value of introducing some business techniques that can be adapted for use in charitable organisations.

This led to an experimental seminar entitled 'Making Boards Effective' under the joint auspices of the City University and Gresham College in 1988. Gresham College is an educational trust which has the Corporation of London and the Worshipful Company of Mercers as its trustees. The success of the seminar led Gresham College to extend their financial support to five further seminars in 1988, and I would like to record here my gratitude for their support and encouragement.

It became obvious that it would be useful to produce a handbook, both for those attending future seminars and for trustees of charities and for others involved in voluntary bodies who might not be able to attend such a seminar.

This handbook is not written from a didactic or authoritative standpoint. It expresses a personal view throughout and seeks to examine the basic principles of how charities and voluntary bodies, such as boards of schools or top committees of any sort, can effectively be managed and the implications of these principles. In addition it offers ways of approaching such aspects as planning from a businesslike point of view.

The diversity of types of charities, the incredible range of their manner of organisation, the vast differences in size, and the extraordinary range of people acting as trustees all militate against a dogmatic approach. The principles, however, are the same across the whole field, and the reader must take what he can and apply it to his own organisation, adopting and adapting where appropriate.

This, therefore, is not a text book. It is hoped that it will help many who are apprehensive about responding positively to a request to become a trustee, as well as many who have already accepted such a position without realising the nature and scope of their responsibilities. If it helps some trustees perform their responsibilities more professionally it will have achieved its purpose.

Finally, I wish to express my thanks to the Chief Charity Commissioner and his staff for support of the seminars and their helpful comments on an early draft of this book, to Tony Pinkney whose valuable business experience helped me in the earlier drafting, and to Frank Wilson who guided my thinking on the subject of volunteers. I must also record my deep gratitude to Jessica Kingsley who has given endless help and advice far beyond the call of duty. Despite the immense help received from these, as well as the many who have passed through the seminars held at the City University, I do, of course, take full and sole responsibility for the ideas expressed.

Chapter 2

Background to Charities

We live in exciting times! This is especially true in the charitable world where big changes are afoot at the time of writing. The charitable world is a large sector: one estimate is that there are about 250,000 charities in England and Wales, with a total turnover of over twelve and a half billion pounds each year.

There may be as many as a million people who are trustees of charities or who are involved in the running of voluntary organisations which are not charities. Legislation is now in preparation which will have a profound effect on the charitable sector, although there is little sign that this is appreciated by the general public yet. The change will take several years to be fully implemented but the old easy ways for trustees and others are coming to an end and a greater degree of efficiency and professionalism is going to be required. Hitherto, apart from the excellent little booklets put out by the Charity Commissioners and their valuable advice when it has been sought, there has been little in the way of guidance through the morass of legal decisions that apply, no clear guidelines for trustees to follow and no professional body in existence to be consulted when a difficulty is encountered.

The aim of this handbook is to help people in the top supervisory bodies of such organisations, such as trustees, to understand what is expected of them by examining their role and responsibilities so that they can become more effective.

Voluntary work is an essential part of the British way of life. It is rooted in a desire to help those less fortunate than ourselves. It may involve the giving of time, effort and creativity, quite apart from money.

Hundreds of thousands of people give countless hours of service in this way every year in this country. It is an important and precious part of our heritage. A lot of the time, effort and creativity so provided is devoted to getting others to give generously to worthy causes.

Some engaged in charitable work have business training, but many have no connection with the business world. Together, the trustees running a charity have to cope with numerous management problems similar to those faced by business people across the country, but often their lack of business training and experience makes it difficult for them to cope with such problems.

In addition to those business management problems, there is an obstacle for the charitable trustee that is unique to voluntary organisations. This concerns the question of how a group of voluntary people manage a non-profit making business *(see glossary)* for which they are deemed in law to be responsible but from which they are not allowed to benefit themselves in any pecuniary form: how they should conduct themselves in a fiduciary capacity as trustees when exercising their management role.

There is a third set of problems that such trustees face: the logistical problems of how, in practical terms, a voluntary body which meets only infrequently can effectively exercise proper control and supervision over those who are employed and working full time in the charitable organisation. One important element of this logistical problem is the fact that control of information is a form of power, and for the top supervisory body to obtain the right information at the right time can be very difficult without the positive help of the full time staff.

These three groups of problems - the need for business/management expertise, the implications of the fiduciary capacity role and the sheer logistical problem of how part time voluntary people can manage fulltime workers effectively are the main issues tackled in this handbook. Training and experience are the two natural prongs of attack on such problems; this handbook attempts the former for those who lack the latter.

Historical background

I am indebted to the excellent booklets put out by the Charity Commissioners from which they have allowed me to summarise the following brief historical outline.

Obviously men have helped each other from the dawn of time, but charity as we might recognise it today in our country started as a religious activity. The Church urged Christians to bequeath their wealth to pious causes. In the Middle Ages, money was given for the reciting of masses for the dead, the repair of churches or religious houses. To this were added the gifts for relief of suffering and poverty, and for hospitals.

Upon the dissolution of the monastries in the sixteenth century, alongside the rise of a prosperous middle class, charity became secularised and schools, almshouses and training for apprentices became common.

Originally charitable bequests came under the jurisdiction of the ecclesiastical courts but by 1500 the Chancellor had assumed jurisdiction. With development of the 'use' or 'trust' *(see glossary)* his jurisdiction became paramount.

There is no statutory definition of the word 'charity'. The legal concept is embodied principally in case law stemming from the Statute of Elizabeth I in 1601. Over the centuries the concept of charity has developed and extended to keep pace with changing social circumstances and concepts of need.

In the early nineteeneth century there was much public concern and discussion about the state of charities in England and Wales. The only remedy when a trust had fallen into the hands of corrupt or otherwise inadequate trustees was for application to be made to the Court of Chancery. A Royal Commission was set up and, following its recommendations, the first Charitable Trusts Act was passed in 1853. This established a Board of Commissioners with a staff of inspectors who had power to enquire into the state of a charity, to summon witnesses and examine them on oath, to give trustees legal advice on which they could rely, to sanction transactions in charity property and to control the bringing of charity lawsuits. The Commissioners reported from the beginning that they found their powers unduly restrictive.

At various times since 1853 the powers of the Commissioners have been extended in one way or another, until, in 1960, a new Charities Act was passed which consolidated all existing charity law and granted further powers. The Charities Act of 1985 imposes a stricter duty on trustees of local charities for the poor in relation to their accounts, introduces simpler procedures for modifying the objects of such charities and for the transfer of property from one charity to another, and enables very small charities to be wound up.

The present position

Over the last half century there has been an explosion of growth in the world of charities. Whereas the old pattern was for most charities to be endowed with funds by the person setting up the trust, in the forty years since the last war we have seen many charities formed with few assets on the basis that they raise their funds from the general public and channel those funds to areas of need. More recently we have also seen huge sums raised through the media - especially television. Some causes now raise massive sums on a world-wide basis in a short period of time.

At the same time, as might be expected, fraud has spread further into the charitable area, and now takes many forms. The media is quick to seize on a charity which, for one reason or another, goes wrong, or which was set up with fraudulent or near-fraudulent intent. As all charitable giving depends on the confidence and goodwill of the public, it is of vital importance that the general perception of charities does not become tainted. This in turn has focused the spotlight on the safeguards that exist or should be put in place. With a total estimated annual turnover in excess of £12,500 million, a very considerable amount of public money is channelled to charities through reclaimed tax, relief to donors and in other ways.

For all these reasons an examination of the existing mechanism of supervision of charities has been taking place in recent years, with a view to passing new legislation if necessary and taking whatever practical steps appear desirable.

A Report entitled 'Efficiency Scrutiny of the Supervision of Charities' (HMSO) was produced by a group, appointed in February 1987 and headed by Sir Philip Woodfield. It gives valuable insight into both the problems and the present position. Together with a Report by the Committee of Public Accounts entitled 'Monitoring and Control of Charities in England and Wales' (HMSO) it is required reading for those who wish to form some estimate of where matters stand and what may become law in the next few years.

The Woodfield Report has been accepted by the Government. About half of its recommendations do not need legislation and it is understood that these are being implemented forthwith. The rest of the recommendations call for legislation which is now in the drafting stage and is to become law by 1991 at the latest.

The crux of the debate is the degree of accountability of charities and how far they should be monitored and regulated, to what degree such regulation should be self-regulation, and the mechanics of how any necessary regulation can be best effected.

The argument in favour of better self-regulation appears to be gaining ground on all sides, but the matter is still not at the centre of public attention and there is some way to go before law is passed.

Whatever happens, it is clearly right that resources should be allocated for the purpose of ensuring that the enormous figure given by the taxpayer to charity is directed efficiently to the right objects. Trustees generally, and particularly those receiving a large amount by public donation or from fiscal privilege, are going to have to bear closer scrutiny of their activities. They are going to have to open up their affairs in a more detailed way to the public, and be more closely monitored and more clearly answerable for their actions. All this adds up to the need for them not only to be more responsible and efficient, but to be seen by all to be so.

Chapter 3

What is a Charity?

Why become a registered charity ?

At present registration with the Charity Commissioners is taken generally to establish the bona fides of a charity. In fact, it only means that the charity has been examined by the Charity Commissioners who, being satisfied that all its purposes are exclusively charitable, have accorded it a registration number. Once it has been registered and given a number, those in the charity will find it easier to obtain gifts of money, goods and services from the general public and from companies and grant-giving charities.

Once accepted by the Inland Revenue (following registration by the Charity Commissioners) the charity can obtain valuable tax advantages and can offer tax incentives to prospective donors. The benefits are subject to change from time to time, but presently include income tax, corporation tax, stamp duty, capital transfer tax and capital gains tax. Local rates relief can also be claimed.

The four main charitable purposes

The whole of the constitution of a new charity is examined by the Charity Commissioners before it is allowed to become a registered body. Four categories of charity are recognised whose purposes cover:

- the relief of poverty
- the advancement of religion

- the advancement of education

- other purposes beneficial to the community

The Charity Commissioners will insist on any new organisation having a written instrument - referred to as the 'governing instrument' - before registration. That governing instrument sets out the constitution and must state the objects which require to be agreed by the Charity Commissioners before the charity is accorded a number and able to start work.

Two main types of charity

1. Unincorporated, which includes associations, clubs, societies, trusts and friendly societies.

   These bodies do not have the same legal existence as limited companies and it follows that the officers may incur unlimited personal liability when entering into contracts. Although they could reclaim from the organisation what they have had to pay out, that may not be of much help if there are insufficient assets.

2. Incorporated, which includes companies (usually limited by guarantee), industrial and provident societies and chartered institutions.

   The incorporated body can sue and be sued in its own name. It has a legal 'life' and can be wound up. It is operated by its directors who are elected (and removed) by its members. Companies and industrial and provident societies also come under special Acts.

Getting the charity moving

One of the first tasks of the trustees is to elect a chairman and a treasurer and, possibly, a secretary. The trustees elect their chairman and

Figure 1: Forms a charity may take

INCORPORATED	UNINCORPORATED
Companies limited by guarantee	Associations
Companies limited by Royal Charter	Clubs and Societies
Industrial and Provident Societies	Trusts
	Friendly Societies

COMMENTS

Are legal entities	*Not legal entities*
Can be sued in their own name	*Cannot sue or be sued*
Members of top supervisory body are only liable personally if they fail to perform their duties properly	*Members of top supervisory body may be fully liable to the full extent of personal assets for the whole debt*

treasurer from among themselves. The effectiveness of the chairman is crucial to the success of the trust. Among the trustees, he is the 'first among equals'.

Creating the ethos of the charity

Once the constitution has been settled and they have elected a chairman and treasurer, the trustees will need to decide what to do. At this moment, as they move into creating an organisation to carry forward the work of their charity, it is appropriate to recognise that each organisation creates and perpetuates its own ethos. This is created by a great number of factors including the rules and type of activity the organisation is created for, the attitude of any staff who are employed, the environment, the personalities of those running the organisation, the standards laid down by the founders, the controls implanted in the systems and the working relationships set up between the staff. Many of the basic rules of conduct - how people will act while at work - fall into place without anything being written down.

Trustees should be aware of this, because they should start as they mean to go on. They need to be aware of the importance of making clear to any staff employed by the charity the standards they wish to set and their desires about what sort of organisation it will be. This is the time to put in place written practices and procedures, and to define the sort of information they require, at least initially, to be supplied to them regularly by the executive officer. If everything is so new that the trustees have no idea what information they will require monthly, quarterly and annually then they should at least make it clear to the staff that information will be needed, and that it will be specified later and that the requirements may be changed from time to time. The importance of the adequacy and timeliness of the flow of information to the trustees cannot be overemphasised and will be explored at length later.

Definition of charities

One of the problems of discussing the charitable field as a whole is that
it is so diverse and so large. Charities range in size from the small and
local to large organisations such as Oxfam. Some charities are endowed
with funds, which they dispense freely, others have to raise every penny
they spend from the public. Some are run by the trustees themselves,
others have hundreds of staff reporting to them through an executive
officer. Some have built up a network of volunteers across the country,
others have only paid staff.

Obviously the range of what may be called 'voluntary bodies'
(which includes charities) is even more diverse. Their activities range
from the board of a school to the committee running the cricket club -
and the cricket clubs range from the local village club to the MCC.
Some organisations seek publicity, others shun it. Some are large, some
are small; some want to expand, others wish to stay exactly as they are.
The scene is kaleidoscopic.

Common factors

There are, however, a number of factors that are common to the whole
field of voluntary bodies. Three of the common factors that underlie
all these are:

1. The organisations are all in the voluntary field - that is they are not
   working with the sole or even principal aim of producing profit.
   Any profit they make through their activities (for example, by the
   sale of a product) is not for distribution to shareholders in divi-
   dends, but for the purpose of furthering the purposes for which
   the organisation was formed *(see page 29)*.

2. Quite apart from the executive officer and all the staff running the
   organisation, both are supervised by a group of people at the top
   of the organisation - the top supervisory body, or board. The
   members of this body are called trustees (in the case of a trust)

or council members, or members of general committee or by some other appropriate title.

3. In the last analysis, these organisations all seek to serve or benefit society in one way or another, usually through an intermediate beneficiary. To a greater or lesser degree therefore in all these organisations a degree of trusteeship characterises those serving on the top supervisory body - they are not there for their own pecuniary profit or benefit.

Amongst this enormously varied group of voluntary bodies there is one particularly large sub-group: charities. Although everyone knows what a charity is, the legal definition of it is extremely complex. For our purpose it will suffice to call it an organisation which is working to benefit others in the interests of the good of society and in which the members of the top supervisory body normally receive no personal benefit. *(See also page 35 and the glossary).*

This handbook deals with problems that affect the whole range of voluntary bodies by looking at the problems that affect charities. It examines how such organisations can be better managed by their top supervisory body which will be referred to henceforth as the board of trustees.

Classification of charities

The usual method of classifying voluntary bodies and particularly charities is by their income or by the size of their assets. There is a third important criterion: number of staff employed, and it is this which is of most importance in the context of this book. It is the presence of paid staff that facilitates the growth of an organisation so that it can achieve its objectives but it is also their presence which radically changes the character of a charity or voluntary body.

In this book we shall be discussing the overseeing of charities in the context of their supervision and management at the highest level,

Figure 2: Classification of charities

No. of staff	Income p.a. Under £100,000	£100,000 to £1 million	Over £1 million to £5 million	Over £5 million
Over 10	A1	B1	C1	D1
1 to 10	A2	B2	C2	D2
1	A3	B3	C3	D3
None	A4	B4	C4	D4

The squares on the diagonal (A4, B3, C2 and D1) represent the most likely categories. As the salary of one member of staff is likely to be at least £8,000 to which must be added numerous other costs (rent, lighting, stationery etc) it is unlikely that there will be many charities in the boxes A1 and A2. For similar reasons it is unlikely that there will be any charities in the boxes C3, C4, D3 or D4.

consequently the size by assets of a particular charity or voluntary body is not particularly relevant here. What is more important for our purposes is income and how many staff there are in the organisation.

This broad categorisation does not take account of voluntary helpers who may be of considerable assistance to the progress of the organisation. However, comparatively few charities are likely to grow to significant size (in terms of income/assets) without at least one paid member of staff.

The main focus for this book is for charities which have not yet grown into the large staff/income categories *(D1 to D4, C1 and C2 in figure 2, page 27)*. A separate section *(page 62)* looks at the special problems that arise in the larger charities.

Crossover points

Most charities set out from small beginnings and take a number of years before they move into the £1 million bracket, or acquire over ten fulltime staff *(C1 or D1)*. While it is hard to define exactly where the it occurs for any particular charity, it can be seen clearly that the largest charities have moved beyond the point where trustees can be involved in the detail of the charity in the way they could when it was small. They have passed what might be called a 'crossover point'. The duties and responsibilities of the trustees do not change in this process of growth - they are the same for the small new charity as for the £10 million charity. The manner in which they fulfil those duties and responsibilities however, has to change considerably as the charity grows.

This problem of adjustment occurs whenever a charity grows. The old methods adopted by the trustees when the charity was small no longer suffice. One of the problems faced by vigorous and growing charities is that sometimes their trustees are trying to exercise their function as if the charity were still small. They have failed to recognise that a crossover point has been reached and passed. In fact, of course, there are a number of crossover points for trustees, which is another way of saying that they need constantly to be aware of the need to adjust their methods of supervision to adapt to the changes in the size and organisation of the charity itself. *(Please see Chapter 4)*.

What is a trust ?

A Trust establishes a formal relationship between three parties. There is an agreement between the **Donor** and the **Trustee(s)** to put into the possession of the **Trustees** money and/or property (called the **Trust Property**) for the benefit of the one or more **Beneficiaries** in accordance with certain purposes (the **Trusts**). The trustees are therefore the nominal owners of the trust property but may not benefit personally from that property while they are trustees (unless the trust deed so allows), and must ensure that it is used solely for the purposes written down in the trust deed. They must safeguard the property as if it were their own, and pursue the purposes of the trust to the best of their ability.

All charities have trustees, who are the persons who have the general control and supervision of the charity. There is a direct obligation to register the charity with the Charity Commissioners in all but a very few cases, and this legally establishes charitable status.

As it is quite usual for the trustees of a charity - especially one which is engaged in a sizeable business venture - to be likened to the directors of a company, it may be helpful to define the differences. It is important that the differences between a charitable trust and a commercial company are fully recognised; sometimes they seem so alike in their activities that similarity is assumed in areas where in fact they are quite different.

1. The first is that the basic objective of the organisation is different. The charity is not for profit, but rather seeks to serve society through helping a particular section of it. In a charity the yardstick of success is how far the trustees have achieved the task laid

Figure 3: The three parties to a charitable trust

DONORS   *may be a single founder donor*
                          or the public through general appeal

TRUSTEES   *manage the trust and are*
                          responsible for it

BENEFICIARIES   *the person(s) or organisation*
                          specified in the governing instrument

Note that both the **Donors** and the **Beneficiaries** may be indeterminate groups of people. The Trustees must be specific individuals but may include an unnamed individual who is defined by his or her office. In the latter case it is important that they signify their acceptance of the role of trustee as otherwise there is no evidence that they have ever taken up their responsibilities, for which they are personally liable. This is usually done by the person appointed as trustee signing the Minute Book at the first meeting of trustees that they attend.

upon them in the governing instrument, which is not always easy to assess.

The company, on the other hand, is in business to make a profit and, while it is to be hoped it has a sense of social responsibility, its main yardstick for success is financial, which is more easily measured.

2. The second difference is that the top supervisory body (for example the board of trustees) consists of volunteers who (unless there is special provision in the governing instrument) are unremunerated. Indeed, the essential concept of charity trustees is that they receive no personal profit or gain for their activities as trustees. They must be 'disinterested' as regards personal gain or profit. The director of a company receives benefit, whereas the motivation of the trustee must be philanthropic.

3. The third difference lies in the nature of the funding. Either the charity will already be endowed with funds or it will plan to raise money in one way or another, so as to provide the service for which it was created. In contrast, the company is funded by shareholders and lenders who expect to benefit in one way or another.

4. The fourth difference concerns accountability. The top supervisory body of a charitable trust is accountable to no one whereas in a company the directors are appointed by the shareholders and report to them. In a charity the trustees assume responsibilities in response to an invitation by or on behalf of the original donor(s) of the funds or by the existing trustees. There is no clearly defined body to which trustees are accountable periodically, although a registered charity is required by the Charity Commissioners to file a report and accounts periodically, and these are open to public inspection. There is no outside body which will meet to consider how the trustees have performed. They are the top supervisory body in a very real sense.

It is necessary to add that the trustees owe a general duty to society or 'the public', as well as the beneficiaries. However, these are indeterminate bodies of people and create a different environment from that in which the company operates.

5. The fifth basic difference between the trustee and the company director lies in the nature of the liability of the trustee. The obligation assumed by a trustee is a personal one and they are liable personally to the full extent of their own assets (*see figure 1*). As trustees they must act in a fiduciary manner. If they fail to do so they become liable to an action against them personally for breach of trust, which is a wide area for attack. On the other hand, the company director (who also has a fiduciary duty) is liable in ways that are set down in statute such as the Companies Act. Although their liability may be considerable it is not, perhaps, as onerous as that of the charity trustee.

6. Finally, the sixth area of difference is legal: the statutes and legislation concerning trusts and trustees are distinct from those concerning companies.

The Constitution

To constitute an organisation means to set it up formally, to give it legal form, to create a structure. The Constitution is the name given to this act which is usually embodied in a document.

An organisation can exist without any written constitution at all. The members agree verbally to act together for a purpose and commit nothing to writing. Furthermore, such an organisation can raise money from the public for a charitable objective, but if they do adopt this method they will be deemed to be a charity in the eyes of the law, and thus come under the obligations of the law applying to trustees and charities. Those managing the charity will be deemed to be trustees acting in a fiduciary capacity. If they overstep the boundaries around that role they lay themselves open to the charge of breach of trust. Not registering as a charity therefore provides no escape from liability for those who misuse the funds placed with them by a generous but naive public.

Most organisations commit their arrangements to writing. This is essential for those organisations that wish to submit themselves to the Charity Commissioners to achieve charitable status, for without some form of written constitution they will not be considered for registration.

Charities might desire to register for various reasons, including:

1. the need to provide conclusive proof to authorities such as the Inland Revenue that the charity has been properly set up, that its constitution has been agreed by the Charity Commissioners, and that through registration it is now recognised at law as a charity.

2. the desire to satisfy substantial donors who usually look to see whether the charity has been registered before considering any sizeable gift. If it is registered it is taken by the public to have the stamp of approval; if it has not been registered with the Charity Commissioners then it is often considered suspect until investigated. Charities seeking donations do not wish to place this hurdle in the way of donors. In fact it is a misconception that registration gives a general stamp of approval - all it provides is conclusive proof that the charity is accepted in law as having only exclusively charitable purposes.

A written constitution is sensible for other practical reasons - it helps to define not only what the organisation is about but also how it will operate. It puts beyond argument the arrangements made, and it sets down rules for those following later in the organisation.

The instrument which constitutes the organisation is usually called the 'governing instrument'. In the case of a trust the governing instrument is the Trust Deed.

Terms of the governing instrument

Sometimes these terms are drawn widely (e.g., 'to help the poor'), sometimes they are drawn very narrowly (e.g., 'to provide a Christmas lunch for widows residing in the parish of Little Holden'). But whether the objectives are expressed in wide or narrow terms, it is the trustees who alone carry the legal responsibility and who hold the legal powers to transact the business of the trust. It is only the trustees who have the ultimate power and the authority to deal with the assets, employ and dismiss staff, determine the terms of contracts and sign them, etc. The governing instrument may lay down a required number of trustees or specify minimum and maximum figures. It will also probably state how many trustees are required to form a quorum. The board must have regard at all times to the number of trustees in relation to the quorum needed to transact business. This is of special concern to the chairman as one of his responsibilities is to ensure the smooth working of the business of the trust. For the same reason he is also concerned to ensure there are sufficient of the right sort of people brought onto the trust as trustees. *(See also Chapter 6).*

When the trust deed (the governing instrument) is being drawn up - usually with legal help - its provisions need to be very carefully considered. Once it has been signed by those agreeing to become trustees, its terms and conditions have to be followed scrupulously by them and their successors. They accept the trust deed as it stands, and (except where the facts would warrant a change called a 'Scheme of the Commissioners') cannot legally complain subsequently that they would have preferred some other arrangement.

The manner in which the organisation conducts itself must be in accordance at all times with the directions laid down in the governing instrument. For the trustees to step outside the terms of the governing instrument is to lay themselves open to an action for breach of trust in which they would be liable to the full extent of their personal assets. A learned judge once said that assuming the office of trustee 'is attended with no small degree of trouble and anxiety . . . it is an act of great kind-

Figure 4: What is a charity?

Definition according to the Charities Act of 1960:
'...a trust or undertaking established for charitable purposes only according to the law of England and subject to the charity jurisdiction of the High Court.'

Key Words

trust or undertaking	*covers many different forms of enterprise*
established	*it must have some continuance. The Charity Commissioners require a written constitution*
charitable	*as defined by the Charity Commisssioners - their acceptance is conclusive proof in law*
purposes	*as laid down in the governing instrument*
only	*must be exclusively charitable, cannot be partially charitable*
jurisdiction of the High Court	*means that the charity property is held by individuals in their private capacity, not public property held by a public authority*

A charity trustee is defined in Section 46 of the Charities Act as someone who, alone or with others, has the general control and management of the administration of a charity.

ness in any one to accept it' (per Lord Hardwicke L.C. in *Knight v. Earl of Plymouth, 1747*).

In all that follows the reader must first pay particular attention to the actual terms of the governing instrument for his organisation, as these will overtake any general advice or guidance given below.

In the case of charitable trusts the trustees have the tasks of safeguarding the assets of the trust, following the directions of the governing instrument, and seeking diligently to achieve the aims for which the trust was set up in the first place. How the trustees should act generally and how they should conduct themselves is now the subject of extensive statute and case law. This handbook does not attempt to give guidance on the legal position and there are a number of books easily available for those who wish to look deeper into these aspects. Instead we shall concentrate on how trustees can become more effective as they work together within the trust.

It is perhaps important to note first, however, that in law trustees are required to act 'properly'. 'Acting properly' has been defined as acting reasonably and prudently in all the affairs of the charity. Trustees must always act in the best interests of the beneficiaries and avoid letting their personal views or prejudices affect their conduct as trustees. They must maintain, in carrying out the terms of the trust, the standard of diligence and care that prudent business people would show in the management of their own affairs. Above all they must recognise that they are in a 'fiduciary' position and are not entitled, unless expressly provided in their governing document, to make a profit or gain a personal benefit. This is best explained by a quotation:

> 'It is an inflexible rule of the Court of Equity that a person in a fiduciary position is not, unless otherwise expressly provided, entitled to make a profit; he is not allowed to put himself in a position where his interest and duty conflict.
>
> - Lord Herschell in *Bray v Ford 1896*.

Lord Cohen said, in *Dale v IRC* in 1954 that it was a fundamental principle of equity law that a trustee cannot receive anything for services except so far as he may be authorised so to do by the instrument creating the trust or by the court. In law, therefore, a charitable trustee is not allowed to put himself in a position where his interest and duty may conflict, and this can even apply after he has left the trust. If a trustee finds a conflict developing he must explain the position to the other trustees and would be wise to seek legal help if the matter is of moment.

It is a requirement of the law that trustees must act together. By this is meant that no single trustee, acting alone and independently, can bind his fellow trustees. They must agree together on what they intend to do, although trustees of charities are in a special position in that they do not have to be unanimous in their decisions. The majority can bind the minority. This should make anyone who is asked to become a trustee first enquire carefully about the standing of their fellow trustees, if they do not already know them personally .

Finally, it is important for charitable trustees to recognise that they cannot delegate the essential element of their work as a trustee to others, although they can employ experts and others who can make decisions on the day to day management. This principle is expressed in *Turner v Corney* (1841) in which it was said that trustees who take on themselves the management of property for the benefit of others have no right to shift their duty onto other persons. If, by reason of the size of the work of the charity, they need to delegate to employees decision making on day to day management matters, then they must lay down clearly the scope of the authority being delegated. Such delegated authority should be laid down in writing and instructions given for decisions on important matters to be reported to the trustees, who remain legally responsible and must supervise and control the work of the officers.

Once the charity is formed, has a constitution and is registered by the Charity Commissioners, it can begin the business of the charity.

Figure 5: Basic relationship of various bodies

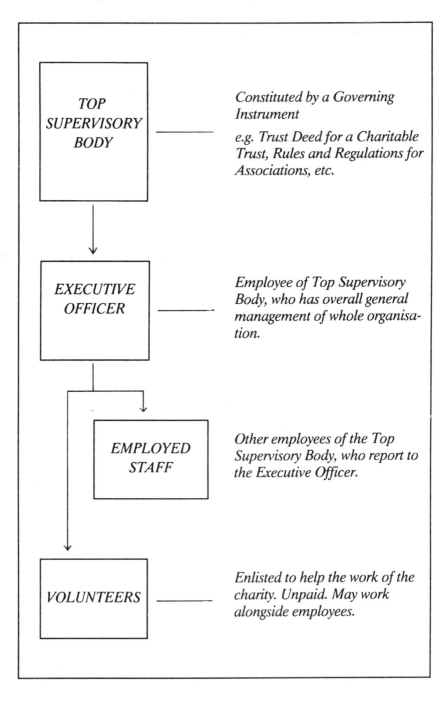

Figure 6: Financial flows

THE CHARITY

Receives assets from donor(s) who sets up the trust

Donations from the general public

Profit from any business conducted

Payment for services rendered

Rent from property belonging to the trust

Interest and profit from investments

Other

Pays expenses (e.g. salaries, rent and administration expenses)

Provides money goods and services for the beneficiaries

Makes other payments and losses (e.g. on investments)

ALL IN ACCORDANCE WITH TERMS SET OUT IN GOVERNING INSTRUMENT

Chapter 4

The Role of the Board

The board of trustees is the top supervisory body of the trust. Whatever name it is known by - be it board, council or general committee - it is the group of people legally responsible for the organisation and it is the body which holds the ultimate power and authority.

The trustees must safeguard the assets at all times, but these should be viewed in the widest possible way:

- **Money**: must be held safely and put to good use (for example, by earning interest when not needed).

- **Other assets:** will include property and equipment. These assets must be safe, insured if necessary and cared for to preserve their value. If the purposes of the trust would be better served by re-investing their value, they may need to be realised.

- **People:** there should be enough staff but not too many, as this would be a waste of assets. They need to be well directed, trained and motivated.

- **Time:** there should be a sense of urgency in the attitude of the trustees. The organisation should have well defined goals for achievement by a certain date.

The trustees have a personal obligation to use the assets within the terms of the governing instrument of the trust for the purposes set out therein.

The Mission Statement

It follows that the top supervisory body must first extract from their governing instrument the purpose(s) for which they exist and then seek to fulfil that purpose by devising plans (long, medium and short term). They will start from the governing instrument and a distillation of what they think their overall task to be, which we shall refer to as the Mission Statement. The main purpose of the Mission Statement is to provide the context for the the task of matching the resources (assets) the trustees already have, or think they can obtain, to the defined aims which have to be achieved in as efficient a way as possible. *(See page 92)*.

The top supervisory body must plan to achieve the aims set for a particular period by using the present and potential assets. It is the role of the top supervisory body to 'make things happen' and unless board members understand and accept their role and responsibilities, and are motivated to achieve the desired result, there will be problems.

Boards with role problems

1) Essential and non-essential functions of the trustees

In the initial phase of the charity the trustees themselves have to do whatever is needed but, in the second phase, when growth has occurred, volunteers and employed staff may take over the operational tasks. Some charities never grow in size beyond the initial phase but most charities endeavour to grow in income, numbers of staff, and in numbers of volunteers.

In the second phase of the life of the charity the trustees release the operational tasks to the staff and concentrate on their essential functions, for which they have a legal obligation. For example the trustees may themselves, in the early days, help to raise donations from the general public - either by donations boxes or by specific requests to selected individuals. Later, however, after the trust has grown large enough to employ several staff and some volunteers, the trustees may

Figure 7: The role of the trustees

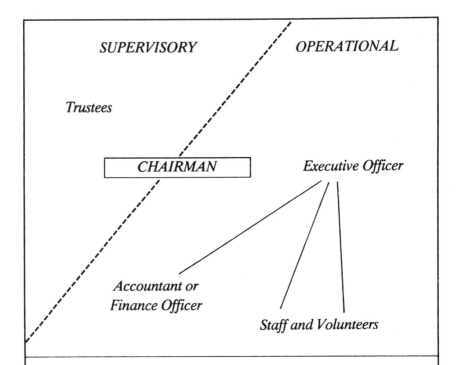

The trustees are legally as well as morally responsible for all aspects of the organisation - supervisory and operational.

The executive officer is responsible to the trustees for the operational side of the charity, including management of the accountant or finance officer.

The treasurer has a special link to the staff dealing with the financial aspects of the charity, but the officers concerned are primarily responsible to the executive officer.

The operational area comes under the control of the executive officer and the trustees must be careful to avoid trespassing on territory delegated to the executive officer, even though their overall authority extends over the whole organisation.

need to discontinue being personally involved in fundraising of this sort so that they can use their time more effectively. They need to recognise the existence of crossover points *(see page 28)*.

The trustees have an essential role (for which they have a legal obligation), but beyond this personally they may assist or not as they choose.

Trustees sometimes experience confusion over their role when they fail to understand that, as their charity grows, the way they can best fulfil their role also changes. Indeed, they must change and adapt to the changing requirements of their charity.

2) *Prestigious trustees*

Confusion about the role of the board can lead to the appointment of prestigious people as trustees. The aim is good: to show the world that people of substance and standing in the community support the work. This is especially important if the trustees are going to appeal to the general public for funds. It seems logical therefore to ask eminent people to become trustees. Unfortunately, such people may lend their name to a number of organisations - maybe even a score or more - and are usually very busy people, quite unable to spare time to attend board meetings or give the necessary attention to the business affairs.

It is preferable to link their name to the trust by appointing them as patrons. As such they lend their name, thereby expressing benign interest and support, with their name shown on the notepaper. An alternative is to make them members of a Council of Reference, or some similar body, which might be called together annually, be given a report on the progress of the organisation and consulted in a general way. The names of the prestigious supporters comprising the Council of Reference can be shown on the notepaper, thereby achieving the desired effect.

Whichever course is adopted, prestigious supporters will be pleased to be released from the burden of many meetings, and this

Figure 8: Prestigious trustees

Solution No. One

TRUSTEES

EXECUTIVE OFFICER and staff

PATRONS
who agree to be publicly
associated with the
organisation

Solution No. Two

TRUSTEES

EXECUTIVE OFFICER and staff

COUNCIL OF REFERENCE
(or similar name)
who agree to be publicly
associated with the
organisation and take some
general guidance/advisory role
through infrequent meetings.

In neither case is the task of the trustees in directing and
controlling the trust interfered with. In both cases the names
of prestigious people who back the trustees of the charity can
be put on the notepaper of the trust.

frees the trustees to be a fully functioning body with all its members exercising their proper role of oversight of the organisation.

3) Dormant trustees

Confusion concerning the role of the top supervisory body can occur when there are dormant or apathetic trustees. This is difficult to deal with and each situation has to be looked at on its merits. One solution may be for the chairman, as the involvement and the number of meetings of the board increase and these trustees find it more inconvenient to attend, to talk with them individually and agree their release upon the next change of trustees. It may be possible for the chairman to shame into activity some of the trustees who do not take their duties seriously enough by asking them privately to undertake a particular task, such as introducing a particular subject for discussion at the next board meeting.

One of the tests of a good chairman is whether he can motivate trustees to take an active part in the board meetings and then combine them into a team so that they can make their contribution and so fulfil their role. One continuing responsibility of a chairman is to help board members to become creative and to take a productive role.

4) Badly briefed executive committee

Difficulties are sometimes experienced because the board is either too large or too irresponsible to address the real issues, or because its members are just unable to attend meetings. One solution in such cases is to form an executive committee or a management committee - it has many names, but the purpose is clear: to transact business efficiently at meetings which are more frequent than those of the board to which it reports. It may also be formed because of the availability of a small group who can be called together by the chairman or executive officer when he has a problem that cannot settled without higher authority.

There is nothing wrong with having a small executive group and it is a worthwhile way of using the sub committee principle discussed on page 52. Indeed, it is sometimes essential to have an executive committee - for example, where the top supervisory body is too large and has become unwieldy. However, confusion can result if the remit, authority and reporting requirements for the executive committee are not clearly laid down by the board. An executive committee can easily become very important and largely fill the role hitherto played by the board. When this happens the board will begin to find itself superfluous. It can become a rubber stamp for the executive committee, where the real decisions are made.

There are several reasons why an executive committee should not be allowed to take over the role of the board:

- If the charity is deemed to require the number of members that serve on the board, then having the decisions made by a smaller group (the executive committee) prevents the minds and experience of all the trustees being focused on the matters to be decided. The larger group, however, will still carry the legal and moral responsibility for the charity. This is clearly wrong.

- An active executive committee can result in the board members feeling isolated and ineffective. They can lose interest if their function is perceived as being merely that of providing an automatic sanction.

- A small committee is less balanced than the larger board, and is more susceptible to domination or persuasion by a dominant chairman, trustee or executive officer.

- A small committee can get too close to the executive officer. The executive officer is always pivotal in the affairs of the organisation and his concern with the achievement of short term targets may not seem a bad thing. The trustees, however, must have a wider horizon and have to bear in mind constantly the medium and longer term aims, and to weigh up how decisions on immediate problems and opportunities relate to those strategic aims.

The functions of the board

How does the board go about its work? The board is comprised of trustees who are both inside the organisation (as its top supervisory body) and yet retain objectivity in that they stand aside from operating responsibility. When there are a number of employed staff it may be that the activities of the trustees are entirely limited to board meetings. It is their function to fill the top leadership role and to monitor closely the use which is made of the power and authority they delegate to the operating staff. *(See page 42)*.

The five main functions

Apart from the leadership/motivational role, trustees have five main functions (all of which will be explored in more detail later):

1. **Initiating** - the creative function: seeing the vision, creating something from nothing - devising the direction in which to go. This may extend into 'doing' when there are no employed staff.

2. **Planning** - the policy forming function: translating the decisions about direction into definite plans.

3. **Supervising/controlling/monitoring** - if there are employed staff the board will delegate power and authority to achieve the plans agreed. If there are no such staff then the trustees will have to execute their own plans (or supervise volunteers). Either way they must exercise their oversight to ensure that the assets are safeguarded and that fraud, error and waste are avoided as far as possible by good systems and good management, and that plans are achieved.

4. **Reviewing** - a careful assessment of its own performance is periodically needed by the board, and this should be as objective as possible. This self checking function applies whether a trust employs staff or not.

Figure 9: Role of the board

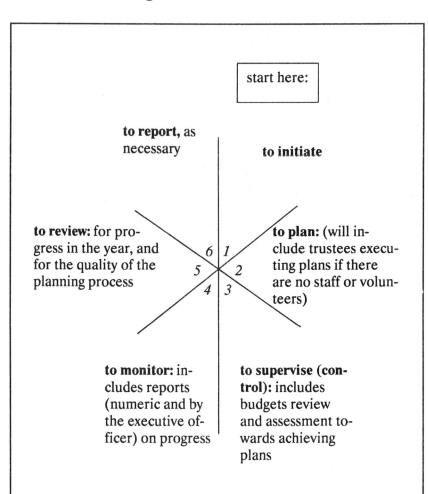

The sequence shows how a charitable trust would start operations.

Subsequently considerable overlap will occur as some of the functions are continuous whereas others are periodic.

Nevertheless the sequence may be of value in showing the logical order of the necessary operations.

Figure 10: Role of the board: initiating

---

1. At the founding of the charity

> definition of the mission statement
>> (as determined from the governing instrument)

> selection of priorities

> assessment of work involved and resources available

> detailed plans to achieve the initial set of goals

> allocation of responsibility

> selection and hiring of fulltime staff (the executive officer and, possibly, certain of the senior staff)

---

2. Subsequently (periodically)

> to reassess the task set out in the mission statement in the light of a changing environment and changing circumstances

> to reassess the present interpretation of the mission statement in terms of goals and priorities

> to assess progress

> to define new aims

5. Reporting - certain reports are required by law (such as financial accounts). Other reports might be desirable but are not legally necessary: donors might need to receive an annual report, beneficiaries might need to be told of the work of the charity.

Frequency of board meetings

A board functions by meeting as often as is necessary to fulfil its obligations. Obviously there can be no hard and fast rule about how often a board should meet - everything depends on the circumstances - but it must meet at least as often as is necessary to pass the resolutions and documents required by law.

Some of the questions that need to be asked concerning the frequency of meetings are:

1. What are the legal requirements for the meetings of the top supervisory body of the organisation? (A company limited by guarantee may be different from a trust established by a trust deed although both are registered as charities.)

   - first meeting within how many months of start?
   - number of times per year?

2. How often do the trustees need to meet in order to perform their basic task?

   - to determine long term strategy?
   - to translate that into medium term objectives?
   - to agree short term targets for the next twelve months with the executive officer?
   - to agree/monitor/review the budget?

3. What are the actual needs of the charity?

   - how often does the executive officer wish to meet the trustees to report and consult?

Figure 11: Role of the board: reporting

Although trustees of a charitable trust are the top supervisory body, and have no body to which they report directly (unless they are, for example, a company limited by guarantee), they are responsible and can be called to account.

There is an obligation on them to report how they have fulfilled the trust reposed in them and for which they are required to act in a fiduciary capacity. They may need to report to:

1. The Charity Commissioners
Should they receive a copy of the annual report?
There may be a legal obligation to submit reports/accounts.

2. The Inland Revenue
Do they need to see the Report and Accounts?
Do they need to see details of convenanted donations etc.?

3. The VAT Authorities
If liable for VAT, certain information will be required at set times by Customs and Excise.

4.The Donors and the General Public
Do they need to publicise their 'results' (i.e. the Report and Accounts) for the benefit of those who have provided resources?

5. The Beneficiaries
Do they need to tell existing or future beneficiaries what they are providing?

6. The Staff
They should consider their relationship with the executive officer and other employed staff to decide whether and how they ought to communicate not only their aims and results (which will supplement action taken by the executive officer) but also to let all the staff know how they are valued by the trustees.

7. The Volunteers
Would it be right to take special steps to let the volunteers know how much their work is appreciated by the trustees? To let them see some of the vision of the future?

- how tight a control (for example, by reports to meetings of the board) does the board desire?

- how often are financial or other issues expected to arise that need the combined mind of the trustees?

- is a special meeting needed each year to review all aspects of the organisation?

Frequent board meetings may be caused by every aspect of the organisation being examined at every meeting. Would it be useful for the board to allocate major reviews of particular areas to specific meetings over the twelve month period? For example:

1st quarter - policy review

2nd quarter - overall financial review

3rd quarter - staff and administration review

4th quarter - budget and planning review

Consider the use of sub-committees of trustees to meet *ad hoc* and make recommendations on specific matters.

The use of sub-committees and executive committees

The burden of a great deal of hard research and thinking can be lifted from the trustees by sub-committees.

This is especially useful for the examination of complex issues. A few trustees are given a clear remit and a date to report back (probably in writing) to the board. The board is then able to digest the report and, by avoiding a lot of preparatory discussion, can get down to the main task of deciding what to do. A sub-committee should not be used to replace due deliberation by the board; the trustees should not delegate their decision making on important matters, not even to a small group of their own number *(see page 37)*. But gathering facts and teasing out the various issues involved can be done more easily in sub-

Figure 12: Frequency of meetings

An example of how subjects for discussion can be spread.

	First Quarter	Second Quarter	Third Quarter	Fourth Quarter
A. Regular Items				
agreement of minutes of last meeting	*	*	*	*
Financial report	*	*	*	*
Review of budget	*	*	*	*
figures	*	*	*	*
B. Non Regular Items				
The Garden Party	*		*	
Sub Committees	*	*		
Annual Meeting			*	*
C. Special Items				
Review of staff and remuneration	*			
Review of policy		*		
Review of administration			*	
Financial review and budgets				*

committee and the results brought back to the board for their consideration.

Large areas of routine work as well as complex issues can be dealt with in this way. Sometimes an 'executive committee' is formed from a few trustees who are able to meet between board meetings and, working strictly along the remit and guidelines established by the full board, ensures that routine progress is made. Such committees can create problems (*see page 46*) but they are often useful and, in some circumstances, essential. In effect they monitor what is happening and, when necessary, take corrective action. They do not initiate new policies. They report back to the next board meeting (to which their minutes have already been circulated) after the executive committee meeting. A committee of this sort avoids the trustees having to delegate more power than they wish to the executive officer between meetings, or having to rely on their chairman being in constant touch with the executive officer to settle problems.

Methods of supervising an executive committee

When a board agrees to set up a managing or executive committee to meet with the executive officer to carry forward the work of the organisation between board meetings, it needs to give careful thought to how that committee should act and report. The following are some initial suggestions.

1. The board must draw up a clear remit for the executive committee and it must

    - specify who should be on the committee, its quorum and possibly appoint a chairman and secretary.

    - give a clear remit of when the committee should meet and what it expects the committee to do at its meetings.

    - specify the powers and authority of the committee, and also probably lay down clear boundaries so that it is clear when a matter is outside its authority and needs reference to the board.

2. The board must fulfil its own planning function thoroughly. It needs to define clearly its mission, its long term strategy, its medium term plans and its short term targets, together with sanctioned budgets for the coming twelve months *(see page 93)*.

3. The board should lay down guidelines for the executive officer and the executive committee in all those areas of the organisation where they are needed.

4. The board must lay down clear avenues of communication - both by requiring copies of the minutes of the executive committee to be sent to each member of the board within, say, ten days of the meeting, and by laying down their manner of communication with the board on certain issues or in emergencies.

5. The board should turn its attention periodically to how the executive committee is performing - probably once a year is sufficient. Is it fulfilling the proper role? Have its decisions been sound? Is it overstepping its authority? If so, how often and why? Does it need clearer or more detailed guidelines? Is board policy clear enough for the executive committee to do its job without problems?

6. The board may decide to write in a degree of flexibility to the authority delegated to the executive committee - for example, by allowing a percentage leeway either side of financial limits imposed in a particular area.

Minutes

However good the discussion that takes place within the board, little may come out of it unless good minutes are produced and circulated

Figure 13: Usefulness of the minutes

1. Communication

The minutes put on record who was present, what business was discussed, what was decided and what action will flow from those decisions. They provide the vital record. They also serve the valuable purpose of communicating what was discussed and decided to those members who could not be present at the meeting.

By agreeing the written record of the meeting all those present unite on the record of what happened of importance and, therefore, cannot dispute them subsequently. They have had their opportunity to correct the minutes, which after approval, stand as the permanent record. Minutes are accepted as *prima facie* evidence in law *(see 3. below)*.

2. Certainty

The minutes are a permanent record and are filed on that basis. This means they can be referred to at future meetings as authoritative. This is one reason why the chairman, after approval at the next meeting, signs the copy of the minutes that constitutes the permanent record.

It is very often the case - such is the capacity between humans for misundertanding - that disagreement arises as to what was actually decided, when it was decided or what next action was agreed.

The written record, once passed at the next meeting, and signed by the chairman, provides the basis for certainty. Any member of the board may ask to see the minute book.

3. Legal

If the decisions of the board of trustees are called into question in any legal matter, the signed copy of the minutes is taken as *prima facie* evidence as to what happened at a meeting.

4. Planning

The minutes form an *aide-memoire* for action to be taken. It is a good idea for the chairman to ask at the end of each item 'who does what next?' and for the initials of the person who should take action to be put in the right hand column.

At the next meeting it is then easy to check that all action has been taken and to see if there are any matters arising.

Many trusts move from meeting to meeting without having much idea about where they are going. They react to events and circumstances rather than plan. Minutes can help correct this by highlighting the next steps to be taken.

5. Reviewing

It is very helpful for the chairman and board members at some point each year to look back over the minutes of the past twelve months to see how the trust is progressing. Often such a review clears the mind for planning ahead.

reasonably quickly. It could be said that a board functions at its highest effectiveness when it understands the need for, and makes good use of, well prepared, timely minutes.

The purpose of minutes is to provide an accurate but concise record of the decisions of the board meeting, together with, if necessary, the salient points made. The closest attention should be given to the taking of good minutes.

The importance of minutes

1. There is an obligation for a proper record to be kept of decisions made, and failure to keep and to approve minutes in proper form would lay trustees open to a charge of negligence. Where the public is being appealed to for donations, the funds must be properly administered and this is an additional reason why the trust must both be properly run and be seen to be properly run. Minutes can be used as evidence that the trustees are doing their job efficiently and effectively.

2. Memories are untrustworthy and the existence of clear and accurate minutes avoids some of the subsequent arguments as to what was actually decided at the meeting. Unforseen consequences often flow from a decision, and it is important to be able to look back in the Minute Book to see precisely what was decided.

3. There is sometimes a conflict between trustees. A simple record of the decisions made clarifies the issue permanently.

4. Trustees come and eventually go, but minutes provide a permanent record.

5. They are a powerful means for ensuring action takes place. The initials of the person who should take action can be placed opposite the item. This answers the simple question: 'Who does what next?'

How detailed should minutes be?

It is usual for minutes to contain a brief mention of the reasons for a decision, but not the whole argument. In a voluntary organisation it may be appropriate for a little more background to be given than in the minutes of, say, a commercial company. For example, it might be useful to record not only that it was decided to terminate the lease granted to the trust for premises in Manchester, but also that those present in the meeting expressed the view that only freehold premises were desirable. No actual decision was taken on the principle, but the consensus of the meeting might be of help in subsequent meetings. The reasoning behind a decision can be of great value to future trustees.

Common faults to avoid

1. The first and main fault seen in Minutes arises from lack of good chairmanship which results in decisions not being clearly reached and/or stated before the meeting moves on to the next business.

2. Sometimes the outcome of a discussion on an issue is left fudged because the chairman lacks the courage to state that two opposing views have not been reconciled. Two strong and contrasting views may have been expressed on a subject, and the atmosphere may have become fraught. The chairman or another member of the board, to keep the peace, comes up with a form of words designed to be acceptable to both sides, but without the issue really being resolved. The words may be deliberately ambiguous so that both sides can accept the compromise, each putting different interpretations on what has been said. The person taking the minutes then finds himself in difficulty. The subject was discussed, opposing views were expressed, but what was actually decided? A good chairman would find a better solution than this - for example, either by appointing a sub-committee to look at the question in more detail, or making sure that, if it is important and the decision can be deferred, it is on the agenda to be discussed

Figure 14: Minutes: common faults

1. Too long
'The matter of the cycle shed was discussed and a lot of discussion centred on how big it should be. Some thought it should contain at least thirty spaces, others thought about fifteen would suffice. After a lot of discussion which went on for a long time it was decided to see how many people brought bicycles over the next few weeks and then to average out the figure and have a shed that size.'

2. Too short
'The decision on the new bicycle shed was deferred to a later date.'

3. Ambiguous
'Some of the committee thought the problem of the bicycle shed size was too big to solve in one meeting. It should be longer. The size was one question and the shape was another - it would need another meeting.'

4. Inaccurate
'Mr Smith proposed that the committee should accept offer by Mr Jones of ...' (but the offer was by Mr Brown and Mr Jones proposed it).

5. Contradictory
'The committee considered that the proposal was unacceptable and should be refused. The chairman said he would speak to Mr Smith. A vote was passed to accept the proposal.'

6. Misleading
'The question of the bicycle shed was not resolved and it was agreed to drop it. The committee went on to discuss...' (but the decision about the bicycle shed was only deferred until more facts were known).

7. Wrong dates
'As new facts were needed before a decision could be reached the matter was deferred until the Autumn.' (But it might be decided before then if the facts were forthcoming.)

8. Bias
'Although it was decided to defer the decision on the bicycle shed until more facts were known, several members of the committee felt strongly that it needed to accommodate at least twenty-five machines.' (When, in fact, the argument was fairly evenly divided.)

9. Fudged
'Some felt that there should not be a bicycle shed while others were in favour of building it immediately. The chairman said he hoped that the next meeting would provide the answer.' (When, in fact, all except one member - albeit a person of very strong views - thought the matter had been decided in favour of building.)

at the next meeting, when there has been time for reflection. The minute taker should not be left to sort out a fudged position.

3. Minutes may go to the opposite extreme from merely recording decisions, and become too lengthy, every nuance of argument being included quite unnecessarily.

4. The minute-taker (or even the chairman), either consciously or unconsciously, sometimes imports a bias into the minutes. Minutes should be as objective as possible: clear, concise and above all, accurate.

Need for timely distribution

Sometimes there is a delay in submitting minutes to board members. After only a few days memories of what was decided at a meeting can become blurred. It is a good discipline, unless there are good reasons for delay, for the minute-taker to undertake to have the draft in the hands of the chairman of the meeting within forty eight hours of the meeting. After the chairman has checked these draft minutes with his own notes of the meeting the as-yet-unapproved minutes should be circulated to members as soon as possible. Sometimes a chairman will hand over his own notes taken in the meeting to the person taking the minutes. A good aim is to have the minutes in the hands of the members of the board as soon as possible, and in any case within ten days of the meeting.

Confirmation of minutes

As board meetings may not be frequent, and trustees do not necessarily see each other between meetings, it is a good idea to send the minutes (unapproved at this stage) to board members with a standard covering letter asking trustees to study them immediately and to notify the secretary (or chairman) by telephone before a certain date (say, ten days after receipt by the board member) if they disagree or con-

Figure 15: Aide memoire for minutes of meetings

Who does what?

Activity	Action By	Comments
1. Draft agenda	secretary prepares	*there should be a deadline for submission of items by trustees*
	secretary sends to chairman	*amends as thinks best but meeting will decide*
	chairman sends to secretary	*in final form*
	secretary sends to trusttees	*in good time for meeting, with any necessary papers*
2. Meeting	Chairman conducts	*has responsibility for ensuring the business of the trust is properly conducted.*
	chairman ensures notes are taken of proceedings	*normally by secretary or by a trustee.*
3. Draft	written up by secretary (or whoever took notes) and sent to chairman.	*best done immediately and sent to chairman within 48 hours*
	chairman vets from his own notes and recollections of the meeting	*must therefore be done soon after the event.*
	chairman amends if necessary and returns to secretary for despatch	*chairman only keeps his rough notes taken at the meeting until the minutes are passed at the next meeting*
	secretary sends out to trustees	*may ask for any adverse response within, say, ten days of receipt*
4. Next meeting	chairman asks for approval by trustees	*after amendment the minutes become the official record, valid in a Court.*

sider that there are serious omissions. Such confirmation does not obviate the need for the minutes to be formally approved (or altered) at a subsequent meeting, but it does give an early assurance that the minutes accurately reflect the decisions reached.

The larger charities

The main focus of this book is upon the small to medium sized charity, and a separate book would be needed to tackle the various aspects of larger charities. This section looks at what is perhaps the greatest problem for the charity that is increasing in size: how the trustees need to change their approach to adjust to growth.

When a charity grows it will sooner or later reach the point where it must increase the number of its paid staff. Hopefully there is, also, a parallel growth in its annual income. In the course of this growth the organisation and the issues it faces become more complex. Quite apart from the problems of an increased number of donations, for example, there is the need for more day to day management of people - staff become a major responsibility, absorbing a good deal of time and effort. Likewise, more complicated policies and plans have to be researched and defined and then approved and communicated. An organisation that could be managed by the executive officer and monitored by the trustees relatively easily when small now requires a considerable amount of administrative care and ability.

Although the overall responsibilities of the trustees do not change in any way because of this growth (apart from the obviously heavier responsibility for more assets and more staff), the way that they fulfil those responsibilities must adapt to the changed circumstances. The trustees will no longer be able to spend time on non-essential activities as all their available time will be needed for essential tasks. But which tasks are non-essential and which are essential?

It is fairly easy to see in abstract that any activities done by trustees that do not need to be done by them should be done by others once the charity has grown to a certain size.

What a trustee needs to do in his charity will change. What are seen as essential tasks at the commencement of the charity may become of secondary importance once the charity has grown to a certain size. It is the case, nevertheless, that many trustees spend time, both in meetings and out of them, on inessentials. Involvement in the day-to-day operations of a charity may be appropriate in the early days while it is small or medium sized - for example in raising initial donations - but become superfluous once the charity has reached a certain size. Their responsibilities can be summarised by stating that trustees need to be fully in overall control of the charity, and to do this they need to maintain effective oversight of the charity. They should be fully aware of all that is of significance in order to ensure they fulfil their responsibilities.

The point at which it becomes necessary for trustees to reassess their role and activities and to relinquish some tasks that are no longer relevant has already been referred to as a crossover point. Beyond each crossover point must come greater professionalism and efficiency from trustees to enable them to fulfil their full responsibilities as trustees of a growing charity.

This means that the need for a true partnership between trustees and the executive officer is as important, if not more important, in the large charity than in the smaller ones. Great attention has to be paid to the provision of the right data at the right time - and not excessive data which can confuse. There also has to be a facility for trustees to obtain answers to valid questions between board meetings, so that they can be fully prepared for the decisions they have to make.

In summary, it is essential that trustees in large charities re-examine their role periodically to ensure that they have not abdicated control to the executive officer and his staff, and that they do have adequate oversight, and a grip on policy and planning. The size of the charity in no way changes their responsibility - it only means that they have to be even more more vigilant to perform their essential function well.

Chapter 5

Roles of Board Members

For the board to function properly it is necessary for the board members to understand their own role in the organisation. We do not live in an ideal world, and these positions cannot always be easily filled by experienced people. Understanding the role they should perform is therefore important.

The Chairman

(Sometimes referred to as the Chairperson/Chairwoman or even as the Chair. The term chairman will be used throughout but the office holder might be male or female.)
The chairman has a key role in the organisation.

- He is unlikely to be unseated for the period agreed for his tenure of office.

- He is in a unique position *vis-à-vis* the other board members; he can, by his style of chairmanship, either inhibit or block what others see as progress, or can give a powerful impetus to new ideas and forward movement.

- His grasp, or lack of it, of the conduct of meetings can lead to heightened interest and enthusiasm on the part of his fellow trustees, or to the most unbearable boredom and frustration.

- His attitude to the executive officer in their contact between meetings is important to the executive officer's motivation.

- His commonsense is essential to efficient despatch of the various matters that arise. A wise chairman can be of enormous benefit to a trust - but it may be sensible, every three or four years, to change even the best of chairmen.

Election of the chairman

The chairman may be described as the 'first among equals' - that is, he is merely one of the trustees who has taken on the role temporarily. It is not an office for life, nor is it the chairman himself who decides how long he will continue in the office; in the absence of directions in the governing instrument it is the trustees who are the arbiters of the length of time he will hold office. The opinion and vote of the chairman has exactly the value of any other trustee's, although he may have more knowledge of a particular situation because of his involvement as chairman. He should have no special influence on what the trustees decide, except that normally he will have a casting vote in the event of a tied vote.

The chairman is usually elected annually by his fellow trustees. His option is to decline to stand for a further term. Good re-election procedures should enable his fellow trustees to replace him before 'creeping paralysis' arises in a chairman who has run out of ideas and motivation, or one who only wishes to preserve the status quo.

The chairman may serve for several years consecutively if elected to do so by his fellow trustees. It is worthwhile instituting sound organisational procedures for replacing a chairman as early as possible so that, when the time comes for them to be used, they are not viewed as personally directed at the holder of the office of chairman. Standing procedures could be adopted by the board along these lines:

'Election to the post of chairman shall be decided by vote each year. Once elected, a chairman may stand for a second and a third* term, but may not serve continuously for a period of longer than three years* without there then being an interval of at least three years.*'

It is also useful to agree that at one particular meeting each year (for example, the last, the first or the October meeting) the chairman will withdraw from the meeting, (often leaving at the end of 'Any Other Business'), thus allowing the remaining trustees to discuss whether they wish to re-elect him for the ensuing twelve months. They may have been well pleased with the performance of their chairman over the previous twelve months, or they may now wish for some reason to have a change of chairman. In his absence they are able to talk freely. One of their number is then deputed by the other trustees to advise the chairman of their decision before the next meeting at which, if there is to be a change, the election of the next chairman can take place. This method also allows any necessary canvassing to be undertaken before the next meeting, thus making for a smooth transition of the office.

Desirable qualities in a chairman

It might be thought that any trustee could perform satisfactorily as chairman. Although it depends on the nature of the trust and the quality of the trustees, it is probable that, in most trusts, not all board members would make satisfactory chairmen. Qualities that might be useful in a chairman include clarity of mind, firmness, humour, ability to listen, tact, willingness for hard work (especially in preparation for meetings) and patience.

---

* The board will need to decide on the figure they wish to appear.

Figure 16: Election of the chairman - for how long?

To agree procedure for election of the chairman address these questions:

1. What should be the normal term of office for a chairman?
It is strongly recommended that the normal term of office should be one year. Allow the good chairman to go for a longer period by permitting him to remain chairman for up to a certain number of years.
Recommended answer: One year at a time.

2. What is the maximum of years you wish any chairman to serve?
A normal period is three to five years, after which someone else is elected into the chair.
Recommended answer: Three years

4. What interval of time before an ex-chairman can be re-elected?
It is quite usual for a similar period of time to be required to elapse before an ex-chairman can be re-elected. Thus if the maximum he could serve is three years, then a three year interval should occur before he can resume the chair. Such an interval might be applied even if he only served for a shorter period.
Recommended answer: Three years

4. Should each member of the board be chairman in turn or will the trustees vote for each new chairman?
The rotational system - whereby each is chairman in turn - is not always appropriate or desirable. It depends on the sort of people that are trustees. It is usually best to vote each year either to continue with the present chairman (if his maximum period is not completed) or for a new chairman.
Recommended answer: free vote usually best.

Role of the chairman

(a) Managing trustees

Before considering the procedure at meetings it is worthwhile remembering that one of the tasks of the trustees is to ensure that the team of people on the the board are of sufficient number: if there is not a quorum the chairman cannot proceed. The chairman, as the person in charge of the conduct of the board, will be concerned to see the appropriate people on the board. He needs to consider their experience, views, abilities, age and any other factors that may be relevant. He needs a 'balance' of trustees to ensure wide discussion and good decision making. With the wrong people on the board, meetings can be a wearisome and fruitless exercise.

(b) Chairing meetings

(i) Agenda

Before a meeting the chairman has first to agree an agenda, incorporating items submitted to the secretary or to himself. If he wishes to relegate some items to the following meeting because of probable lack of time he can so indicate, but when it comes to the meeting itself the trustees have the right to call for changes, additions or deletions to the agenda, and their vote on the matter will be final.

(ii) Calling the meeting

The chairman must ensure that the secretary calls the meeting properly, sending out notices in the correct way to the correct people, allowing adequate time before the date of the meeting.

(iii) Providing information

The chairman has to ensure that the members of the board have enough of the right information before them at the right time to discuss the items on the agenda properly. If he considers, for example, that it is essential that they have certain statistics before them to decide a matter then he must ensure that such information is either sent out in advance to them or is provided at the meeting.

(iv) Procedure

The chairman must follow the proper procedure for the conduct of any meeting. It is a prime duty of the chairman to ensure that everyone has a chance to speak and to put their views. Every trustee should feel completely free to contribute on any subject if they consider they have something worthwhile to say. It is precisely at this point that the performance of any chairman can move into the class of excellence. To coax views and opinions out of those who might otherwise to be too timid to voice them, and thus to stimulate profitable discussion, is part of the art of good chairmanship. That art also includes controlling those who want to talk endlessly or wish to try to impose their views on others.

(v) Focus

While it is fatal for the chairman to shut people up too quickly, it is equally frustrating for board members to know that endless discussion will be held about every single point raised. Nothing is more destructive of interest and creativity. Boredom sets in and trustees start to miss meetings. The chairman must keep the discussion centred on the subject before the board.

(vi) Momentum

The chairman also must create and sustain momentum. It is the chairman who has the prime oversight of that most precious commodity: time. He must set the pace, and sustain the vitality of the meetings and, hopefully, the forward movement of the organisation. Unless the chairman is thoroughly on top of the agenda, and knows, for example, which items are going to require more time for discussion, which will need a difficult decision and which items are sensitive to which people, the meeting will be badly directed and likely to meander along inconclusively, either running over the scheduled time or leaving items deferred to the next meeting.

(vii) Direction

The chairman needs to have a sense of direction. It is sometimes a good idea for the chairman to arrange for each agenda to have an item 'chairman's remarks' as a first or an early item. This enables him to point out to the meeting the main items in the agenda which, in his opinion, will need deep consideration and time, and to ensure that everyone can remain until the target finishing time. In this way those present can focus their thoughts and comments on the important items. But the sense of direction needed is greater than just managing the meetings - a good chairman also needs a sense of where the trust is going in its work of accomplishing the remit set out in the governing instrument.

(viii) Authority

Through all these activities the chairman must command respect. He will do this by the manner in which he conducts the affairs of the trust, by his personal relationships with the trustees and others, and by his own integrity and ability.

(ix) Planning

One of the most important requirements of the chairman is that he should put planning firmly on the agenda and in the forefront of the minds of the trustees. If the board fails to plan the whole organisation will suffer and may remain static. (This subject is dealt with in more depth in chapter 7 on page 91).

(x) Intermediary

The chairman is the person who must thoroughly understand the problems facing the executive officer and the realities of the situation so that he can prevent his fellow trustees deciding on some action that is unworkable. He should always ensure that the executive officer is listened to carefully by the trustees.

(c) Between board meetings

Between meetings of the board it is the chairman who represents the board, unless special provision is made. Normally he will represent the board to the executive officer between meetings. He will be the one who is in contact with the executive officer, advising and settling problems if they need attention. This will mean that it is the chairman who, in board meetings, has an especial understanding of the problems faced by the executive officer.

(d) Representing the Board

It is usually the chairman who represents the views of the trust to the outside world between meetings. If the media give some attention to the work of the trust this is usually referred to the chairman who is regarded by the public as having the authority to speak for the trustees. It may be however that the trustees appoint and brief someone else (who may or may not be a trustee) to deal with the media.

(e) Dealing with matters outside his discretion

If a matter arises that the chairman considers is outside his authority - or has been defined previously by the trustees as a matter that they wish to have referred to them - he may contact the other trustees for their advice and help. He may call a special meeting of trustees to enable them to give due consideration to and to deal with the matter, thus ensuring that the trustees move together. In most cases the board will be content to leave it to the discretion of the chairman whether he deals with the matter himself or refers it to some or all of the trustees for discussion and decision.

(f) Executive committee

Often it is the chairman who is involved, along with the treasurer and secretary and executive officer, with meetings of the executive committee between meetings of the board. The terms for such a committee should be laid down by the board in each particular case. *(See also page 45)*.

(g) Overall authority

The chairman should consider himself responsible for the general health of the trust. In particular he will be concerned with the overall safety of the assets, the observance of statutory and other requirements, the smooth functioning of the board of trustees and the momentum of the work of the trust in fulfilling the aims set down in the governing instrument. Although, of course, all trustees are equally responsible for the wellbeing of the trust, the chairman accepts prime responsibility for the overall, continuing progress of the organisation. One reason for this is because, unless there are other arrangements, it is the chairman who is the nexus between the board and the executive officer. He must have his finger on the pulse of the organisation and be the person who receives and passes on information. He needs to have a good relationship with the executive officer. It is normally, therefore, the chairman who is closest to what is happening in the trust.

The Treasurer

The treasurer is the guardian of the finances of the trust, and is responsible for ensuring that there is a proper oversight of finances. He has a watching brief over all aspects: the recording, control and proper reporting of all transactions, the safeguarding of the assets (especially money in whatever form), and ensuring that all expenditure is for the charitable purposes for which the trust was formed and that the general level of efficiency is satisfactory. Obviously he cannot do all this work himself, except possibly in the smaller charities. When others become involved, he needs to be satisfied that those performing these tasks have adequate systems of control and that there are adequate internal audit checks in force. It is not necessarily his responsibility to raise

Figure 17: Lines of responsibility

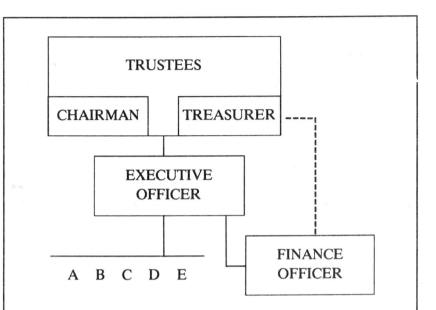

The person in charge of finance (shown above as the finance officer) may be an experienced senior person or he may be merely a bookkeeper. Either way he reports to the executive officer.

The treasurer of the Trust will have a special line of communication to the finance officer, as he will need to ask for figures, explanations or action from time to time.

If problems arise because the finance officer is reporting to the executive officer but taking 'instructions' from the treasurer, the finance officer must first discuss it with his boss - the executive officer. The executive officer may be able to find a solution himself, one way or another, but if he cannot he will then need to mention it to the chairman. It is important that trouble in relationships in this area is dealt with firmly and quickly - usually by the chairman.

The chairman may be able to sort out the problem, one way or another, but if not then he will need to bring it before the next board meeting. Before doing that he will probably have discussed it with the treasurer to understand the issues involved better and to see whether the matter is purely administrative or whether it has deeper roots.

funds for the trust - this may, for example, be the responsibility of a fundraising committee.

In a charity of any reasonable size budgetary systems will be laid down, and the treasurer will be concerned particularly with these and with the supply of information to all the trustees. It is also his responsibility to ensure that each trustee understands the financial figures he places before them, and that they have sufficient information on which to make decisions.

The trustees are entitled to rely on the treasurer for information, guidance, and assurance that financial matters are being managed satisfactorily, but they are not thereby absolved from responsibility. Each trustee is responsible for all the affairs of the trust, and each must judge from the quality of the financial information provided, and by the answers to their questions, whether the financial aspects of the business of the organisation are being properly managed. A trustee must insist on getting answers to his questions if he considers the matter important.

When the treasurer reports to the board he must ensure that enough financial information is given for a proper assessment to be made of the full financial position of the organisation. This responsibility to ensure that all the information is available, and in a form that can be readily understood by those trustees who are not financially trained, is often ignored. A treasurer should explain the figures so that all the members of the board may join in a discussion on the financial implications. It is not good enough for some trustees to opt out of financial decision making, leaving it to others who appear to be better equipped to understand and decide. The treasurer needs to be equally informative and helpful in explaining the financial complexities if he has to report to any other meeting - such as an annual general meeting of a company limited by guarantee.

Role of the Treasurer

a) General responsibilities

- The treasurer is responsible, as are all the trustees, for proper stewardship of all assets but, by virtue of his office, carries an especial responsibility for the cash and financial assets.

- The treasurer communicates (often directly) with employed (or volunteer) staff engaged on financial matters, although they continue to report to the executive officer.

b) Special responsibilities

The treasurer has special responsibility for

- ensuring that the other trustees are made aware of necessary financial information, and that this is presented in a comprehensible way.

- ensuring that any necessary Returns/Balance Sheets/Reports are finalised and filed on time. Care is needed to fulfil statutory requirements.

- ensuring that a sound financial stance is maintained at all times.

- ensuring that auditors are appointed if appropriate. It will be necessary to have professional auditors if the trust deed so stipulates or if the charity comes under the Companies Acts or certain other Acts. In any case it is wise to have any charity, however small, audited by some independent person. If large sums are involved trustees would be well advised to call for a professional audit.

Trustees' responsibility for financial overview

There is a tendency, which is perfectly understandable but which must be resisted, for trustees who have little or no business experience to say, as regards financial matters, that they will rely on the opinion of the treasurer and chairman.

This tendency must be firmly resisted for the following reasons:

- because each trustee carries a personal responsibility and cannot offload this onto the treasurer and/or the chairman. Each must endeavour as best they can to understand the financial issues of each decision before and at the meeting.

- because it lays too great a responsibility on the chairman, treasurer and those other trustees brave enough to admit to some understanding of financial matters.

- because it devolves too much power into the hands of the treasurer and chairman - they can assume too powerful a role and in effect can become an inner control group.

- because if some exclude themselves from discussion, this creates a pressure on those who are prepared to make decisions to settle the issue(s) quickly and move on to matters in which all can join. This does not encourage the best decision making.

- because the minds of all of the trustees are needed in the decision making, not just some of them.

- because those who never grapple with the financial issues can rapidly become disillusioned with their role in the charity and lose interest or feel they have become second class citizens.

- because, finally, it exalts financial matters into a mysterious area, which is wrong. A treasurer should demystify the subject and clarify the issues so that all trustees can understand the options, the implications and the merits and demerits of each.

A treasurer who is good at his job will be able to analyse the financial position to a point where it is simple and clear enough for every trustee to understand, however unaccustomed to business they are. It is up to him to put the financial realities onto paper in a clear and understandable fashion, so that all can appreciate the financial implications of the various choices of action before the board meeting.

If the treasurer is not explaining the financial position clearly to all trustees in this way the chairman (and the other trustees) must persuade him to rectify this. Regular figures should be circulated on paper well before the meeting so that all have time to study them. The significance of changes should be clearly spelt out and the relationship between various figures or groups of figures, when relevant, explained so that each trustee can see their significance. If an important financial decision is going to be faced at the meeting, the preliminary papers can detail the problem, list the options and show the implications of each so that trustees have time to familiarise themselves with the figures and the issues.

The chairman should refuse to proceed with any financial matter of any importance until he is sure that he himself and every single one of the trustees really understands the position, so that all can give informed and serious consideration to the issues to be debated.

To some readers this will hardly seem worth saying but to others it may seem like a counsel of near-unattainable perfection.

Not every charity needs detailed budgets - but it would be wise to assume that your charity is one that would benefit unless there are very good reasons against their adoption. The treasurer should be well versed in how these are managed. It is important to note that timing is of great importance. It may take a large part of the previous twelve months to get well prepared budgets examined, discussed, amended, re-examined, passed and implemented.

The Secretary

A trust does not have to appoint a permanent secretary to the trustees, and often one of the trustees in the meeting will act as secretary and assume responsibility for the minutes. Sometimes a Minute secretary is appointed purely to deal with the minutes.

The tasks that have to be done, either by an appointed secretary or by a trustee acting as secretary, include:

Figure 18: What is needed of trustees

---

1. Attendance at Board meetings

Regular attendance at meetings. Arrive on time and try to avoid leaving early.

Read papers sent out beforehand

Avoid irresponsible questions, suggestions and ideas.

Listen carefully to what others say.

Be practical.

Remember to heed the chairman.

Put enough weight on the views of the executive officer.

Have the courage to be a lone voice if necessary.

2. In relation to employed staff and volunteers

Avoid interfering in the areas of responsibility of the executive officer (either intentionally or unintentionally).

Tell the executive officer your impressions of any visit to the premises of the organisation.

Ensure that all your requests for information are valid.

Try not to cause unrest amongst the staff.

3. Relationship with the chairman

Be creative as regards your input of all sorts (agenda, discussion, brainstorming).

Be ready to give the chairman wholehearted support during the intervals between meeings.

Take responsibility when so asked (e.g. to serve on sub-committees, etc.).

Be part of the team.

Be as objective as possible - and hold onto your own views.

Try not to be negative - there are always a hundred reasons for not doing something.

1. sending out notices for meetings, and other information.

2. receiving suggestions for the agenda from board members and preparing the agenda, conferring with the chairman on the form and content of the agenda, and despatching it to board members along with any relevant papers.

3. taking notes at the meetings of the board.

4. submitting draft minutes to the chairman and, after his agreement, sending the minutes out to all board members for comment and approval at the next meeting.

5. submitting any official returns the Trust has to complete, undertaking correspondence as directed, and holding the Minute Book and other official records.

The ordinary board member

Each board member has equal voting rights. Unless otherwise directed in the governing document the chairman has a casting vote in the event of a tied vote. Most boards tend to operate by consensus rather than by having frequent votes, but each board of trustees will decide for itself how it wishes to operate. Obviously a vote may be called for if a matter is hotly debated, or if a statutory report is being approved.

Each board member is a potential office holder. Board members get to know each others' strengths and weaknesses well in the course of time, and this is of great help when they come to consider who of their number would perform well as the next chairman.

It is important for board members to attend meetings with regularity otherwise they can lose the thread of continuity, and their being out of touch on matters can disrupt subsequent meetings. Absent members, of course, need to be fully apprised of decisions and the reasons behind them, bearing in mind that they are bound by a majority decision. The minutes normally serve to keep absent trustees in the picture. A dissident board member is entitled to have his disagreement recorded in the minutes if he so wishes.

If for any reason a board member cannot attend a board meeting he should let the secretary or chairman know as soon as possible so that, if there will not be a quorum of members, the meeting can be rescheduled. He may be asked his views on certain items which are on the agenda for the forthcoming meeting although, of course, he does not have the advantage of hearing the views of the other members of the board.

Often the date of the next meeting is fixed at the end of the board meeting, but the danger is that a date may be agreed which proves to be impossible for an absentee trustee. When the same thing happens at the next meeting that trustee begins to slip further and further out of touch with what is happening on the trust. The chairman needs to ensure that absent trustees are contacted before the meeting to ascertain their availability for the subsequent meeting. It is a good idea, if it can be done, either to fix a regular date (e.g. second Tuesday of each month) or to fix a list of dates for the whole year at the January meeting.

A board member should study carefully any papers sent to him before the meeting, along with the agenda. By thinking a little about the subject he may be able to formulate some pertinent questions and, perhaps, a preliminary opinion. If he has a question he must ensure that it is really necessary and relevant, and will not waste the time of the meeting.

At the start of the meeting he may wish to propose further items for the agenda, but the chairman, subject to the decision of the meeting, may relegate the item to 'any other business' which means it will only be considered if there is time available at the end of the meeting. If time does run out it is open to the trustee to suggest an extra meeting, or that the item should be put high on the agenda of the next meeting. He has his opportunity to persuade the other trustees, but if they do not agree with him then he is bound by the decision of the majority.

At the meeting of the board he should attempt to follow carefully the facts presented and the arguments advanced. He should try also to put himself in the shoes of employed and volunteer staff to see how the decision would affect them and whether the way forward being suggested is feasible. He should watch for a tendency in himself, and in the other board members, to procrastinate - for example by referring something back on some point of detail - instead of grasping the nettle and making a decision.

Between meetings, the chairman may contact him for his advice or help on some matter. It is his responsibility as a trustee to help the chairman in every way in his power at such times. However, a trustee on such an occasion may feel that he cannot reach a decision on the question with the chairman until he hears the views of his fellow trustees. He may wish to have further facts, or to hear the matter debated. While he will wish to help his chairman, he will have to suggest that, if a decision cannot wait until the next scheduled meeting, a special meeting of trustees should be called.

The chairman, or his fellow trustees at a board meeting, may ask him to serve on some sub-committee to the board, or on some working party. If so, he should do all he can to make himself available in order to further the purposes of the trust.

If the board member is an expert in some field he may well be asked to pay particular attention to that aspect of the work of the organisation. In addition to being a trustee, he then wears the hat of special adviser to the board on that aspect. This does not reduce the responsibilities of the other members of the board in that area - all trustees are fully liable - but they have the benefit of his ability or experience.

The Executive Officer

(see Chapter 8, page 110)

This post goes by many different names, including chief executive officer, director, clerk, manager, general secretary and secretary. The executive officer is wholly responsible to the Board, which appoints him and which is his employer. Because he is a paid employee he does not have the same responsibilities as the trustees themselves, nor does he stand in the same legal position as the trustees. His task is to manage and administer the organisation (including staff) under the direction of the board, and to accomplish the aims they have determined for him. He is in the same legal relationship to the trustees as any other employee.

The executive officer will usually be asked to attend the meetings of the trustees, although some boards will have an occasional meeting where he is not present. Sometimes the executive officer is asked to attend for a part of the meeting only. His input as 'head of operations' is vital and his well-informed opinion on every matter will be depended upon. The ultimate authority and the power, however, reside in the board of trustees and he does not have a vote in their deliberations. Although he has no vote, in the last resort he does, of course, have the option of resigning, but things have come to a sad state if he has to consider this course.

Chapter 6

Selecting Trustees

Selection of trustees

One of the difficult tasks faced by trustees, and perhaps particularly by the Chairman who is concerned to ensure progress, is how to find the right people to come onto the board as trustees.

What are the qualities needed in a trustee? Trustees must be responsible people, for they have to take important decisions and must give due weight and consideration to all aspects of a matter before reaching their decision. It follows that there may be a danger in having as trustee someone who is seriously biased in respect of some aspect of the work. The ideal is a person with a mature, balanced viewpoint and attitude. The longer they remain a trustee, the greater their experience of the organisation, how it works and of the people working in it.

Trustees need to be people with enough time to attend meetings and to help in other ways when necessary. How much time this involves depends on the circumstances of the charity. What part of the day they are free can be important - would they be available to attend board meetings in the middle of the day?

Whether they are willing to spare the additional time needed, apart from meetings, is important. Will they be able to afford the time needed to study important papers prior to the board meeting? They may be called upon to give time, effort and ideas outside meetings. Are they needed to join smaller groups, either to further the work of the organisation (for example, in its early stages of growth) or to discuss and make recommendations on certain matters to the next board meeting?

Do they get on with others? Are they willing to be part of a team? Can they learn from opposite viewpoints and be flexible in theirs? Could they be a future chairman?

Are they needed because they could bring a particular skill or experience to the group of trustees? Do they still have the desired skill? Would they be willing to be useful in this way?

Above all else is the question of their commitment. Do they have the motivation to put real effort behind this charity? Do they really want to give time and effort? Would they only accept because they are friends of the chairman, some other trustee, or the executive officer? Do they really want to come on the board?

It is clearly important that trustees should have some idea of what is expected of them. Is the organisation just starting out? If so, there may be a considerable amount of fairly mundane work to be done - perhaps addressing envelopes and monitoring replies. Is the prospective trustee prepared to share in this sort of activity? Certain charities *(see page 63)* may need a lot of such help from their trustees for a year or two until they become established and can afford to employ staff. On the other hand if a charity has two hundred staff and a good cash flow, with a thousand volunteers, the trustees will be called upon for different abilities and experience.

Are they willing to serve for a period of years? Are they likely to be available for the next few years? Are they often abroad or otherwise unavailable?

Enlisting retired people

Retired people are often the most eligible to become trustees, and there are several powerful points in their favour:

- they have the time available, and can also attend meetings held during the day.

- they are often mature people who wish to use their free time in retirement for a really worthwhile purpose.

- they may have learned through long experience to get on with others, to listen to the other side in an argument, and to come to a reasoned conclusion.

- they will normally be those who enjoy working with other people of the same sort as themselves (mature, experienced, retired), especially if it calls for infrequent meetings and for not too much sustained hard work.

- they are normally financially secure and so can give their time for expenses only.

- often they have some experience of and enjoy committee work.

- they are settled in one place - their retirement home - and are likely to be available for some time.

- if they are being recruited for a particular skill, they have probably had years of experience acquiring that skill.

For all these reasons retired people are the obvious first choice - if they can be found! Especially valuable are those who have retired early and who are looking for something worthwhile to do, as they still have energies to harness.

There may be, however, a 'downside' to having older people as trustees:

- they may be more cautious than younger people - would that be a drawback? It is true that some older people settle more easily for maintaining the status quo.

- they may like peace at any price and therefore be unwilling to argue in the board meeting for what they think is right.

- they may wish to avoid disagreeing with neighbours who are also on the trust, or with others from the same area.

- they may bring the concepts and ideas of yesteryear instead of vital new ideas and outlook.

- they may have run down intellectually or be low on creativity. They may not have much 'attack'.

- they may merely be satisfying their own desire to feel needed, and not really care about the objectives of the charity.

In no way are any of the above points to be taken as automatically true of older people, in which category I place myself. This is merely a list of the possible disadvantages to consider when older people are being considered for the role of trustee. Each eligible person, young or old, must be assessed on his or her own merits. It is reported that the majority of trustees in England and Wales are white, middle-aged or older, and male.

One reason retired professional people are in demand as trustees is that their presence suggests that the necessary business procedures are both known and, probably, observed. Often large organisations (for example, clearing banks and large commercial/industrial companies) have an arrangement whereby staff who are retiring (especially early) can be told of the needs of charities for trustees and/or staff. Some also second staff either mid-career or pre-retirement.

Questions when considering whether to appoint trustees

The first question to be asked before inviting people to become trustees is whether the trust already has enough trustees. If there tend to be problems getting enough trustees to form a quorum then it seems likely that there is a need for one or more new trustees, assuming the governing instrument of the charity so permits. It is possible to have too many trustees - most experienced board members would probably say that ten was a more than sufficient number.

The second question concerns the existing board of trustees - is it a 'balanced' group of people? Does it lack any particular special expertise that would help the trustees in their deliberations? What is the average age of the present trustees - and the age of the youngest and the oldest?

If, for example, the trust administers help to the widows of Nether Wallop it may not greatly matter that there are no trustees under the age of sixty. But if the trust is aimed at supporting a thrusting new activity and needs new ideas and sustained hard work, there should probably be at least a few younger people as trustees. Age is not necessarily linked to creativity, of course, and many retain this capacity into their eighties and beyond. Nevertheless a balance of ages between the trustees is desirable, especially in new and buoyant trusts.

Dangers to be avoided

It is important to recruit impartial trustees. The mistake so many fall into is to ask their friends to become trustees simply because they are friends, and sometimes the friends accept as a demonstration of loyalty. Friends may be the right sort of people to act as trustees but, even if they are, the danger is that they will start with a bias in favour of the person who recruited them.

It is obvious that people who cannot be trusted to keep the affairs of the board of trustees completely confidential should be ruled out immediately, however fitted they may be otherwise. The affairs of the trust are private and all must accept and respect this.

Questions to be asked by a prospective trustee

A prospective trustee needs to assure himself on certain matters before he can allow his name to go forward. Here are some suggestions of the sort of questions that might be considered:

1. Obtain a copy of the trust deed (or other governing instrument):

   - is it clear?
   - what are the objectives and are they all fully acceptable?

- are you willing to sacrifice time, effort, money and even, if affairs went drastically wrong, your reputation for these objectives?

2. Obtain the latest Report and Accounts or whatever official statement exists:

  - how old is it?

  - what financial position does it show? If you are unfamiliar with financial statements of this kind, ask a friend or adviser who knows something of finance and is not involved with the organisation to explain and assess it for you.

  - list the questions that arise in your mind and get answers to each from the chairman or the treasurer of the charity that wishes to recruit you.

  - is the trust viable in a business sense?

3. Obtain a list of the names of the trustees and any other information available about them.

  - are any other people being approached to consider becoming a new trustees?

  - who is resigning?

  - what do you know about each of the trustees? Do you need to know more to be satisfied that they are people you wish to be teamed up with?

  - do you trust their judgement?

  - do you want to work with that group of people?

  - are you willing to be bound by their majority decision if you are in the minority?

  - is it possible to meet the other trustees before deciding? (Sometimes prospective trustees are asked along to a meeting - see whether this is possible.)

4. How do the present trustees see their objectives?

- do you agree that their views interpret the objectives set out in the governing instrument?

- if not, are you going to be a lone voice - how different is your difference of view? How important is the difference?

- do you agree with the priorities of the present trustees, and how important are any differences between their priorities and yours?

5. What sort of time commitment has been suggested to you as necessary by the person recruiting you?

- do you fully realise and accept what the time commitment will mean?

- have you asked whether the work of the trust is about to change - will it require more work/time?

6. Are you content with the professionalism of the charity?

- can you see some of their Minutes? (this may be difficult as minutes are normally confidential).

- how well briefed on your questions is the person who is now recruiting you?

- how much does the whole set-up impress you?

- can you visit the offices/premises where the fulltime staff and/or volunteers work before making your decision?

7. What exactly is expected of you?

- do they need your expertise - if not, why were you approached?

- can you fulfil their expectations?

8. How long are you expected to serve for?

- has any period of service been suggested?

- how long have the present trustees served?

- will it be difficult to find your replacement when you wish to resign in due course?

9. How far are you succumbing to flattery?

- often it is an honour to be asked to be a trustee - are you responding to that rather than the hard facts? Are you really the right person, and have you enough resources of time, energy and money to take it on?

Chapter 7

Planning

Planning is essential in all organisations and is basic to all human life. A decision not to plan formally is in itself a plan. Planning is perhaps the most important single task of the board of trustees. Without effective planning an organisation often either moves from crisis to crisis or simply meanders aimlessly.

Planning consists of a number of elements. These include the quality of the research done, the soundness of the judgements made on the available data and the mechanics of managing the planning process itself. It is therefore clear that a board may exercise excellent judgement but if the research has been done inadequately the results may well be poor. Likewise, the research and consequent judgements may be excellent, but if the planning process itself is performed badly (for example, if the plans are agreed at the wrong time, or if interaction between different plans is not taken into account), then the results may well be poor.

In a constantly changing world survival as well as success depends on planning and the ability to react positively to opportunities and threats. The better the quality of the planning (in all its aspects), the greater the chance of success.

Planning for corporate needs is in many ways similar to planning for charities and other voluntary bodies, but there are also some important differences. One difference is that it must not be assumed in charities that growth is necessarily either essential or desirable. It may be appropriate to try to maintain the existing size of a charitable organisation (by whatever criteria that is measured). It must be remembered that a charity is, essentially, a service to society. The beneficiaries may be very few, and will be only a tiny fraction of society, nevertheless the objective of the charity is to benefit society.

In commerce the competition for markets, and therefore for profits, often dictates growth by which a company hopes to avoid, amongst other things, being swallowed up and losing its identity through take-over by competitors. Such forced take-overs can never happen in the charity world since no one can interfere with the trust, provided the trustees do their job properly. Many, though not all charities operate in a competition free environment as regards their services. However, many charities are seen as competing with each other for donations.

There are many ways to plan successfully, not just one. The planning framework for the voluntary sector shown below is basic in design, but can be applied to all forms of voluntary organisation including charities. At the very least it will provide a starting point.

The mission statement

This is a statement of the overall objectives of the organisation by the trustees and is primarily for the use of the trustees. It is based on extracts from the governing instrument. Sometimes the trustees may find it appropriate to make part or all of the document available to the staff and, possibly, the public.

Ideally, the mission statement is expressed in the words of the governing instrument itself. In a charitable trust, for example, it would be taken from the trust deed. Simply copying the exact words may not be adequate if obscure legal language is used in the deed, or if the wording is not clear. The mission statement should express in clear, modern, non-legal language the objects of the trust; it is not therefore a document that changes often, if at all. In addition to the extract from the governing instrument (expressed in everyday language), it may be advisable to add some sentences to explain and to expand on what

Figure 19: Planning

I The Mission Statement

as set out in the governing document

STRATEGIC
PLANNING

II The Long Range Strategy

need to ask the question:
'Where do we wish to be in the next
five to ten years?'

III The Medium Term Plan

need to ask the question:
'What definite objectives must we achieve
in the next three years to be on course for
our long term plan?'

OPERATIONAL
PLANNING

IV The Short Term Plan

need to ask the question :
'What goals must we achieve in the next
twelve months in order to be on course for
our three year objectives?'

those basic objectives have been taken to mean hitherto. Any clarification that has been obtained by the trustees at any time from such people as lawyers, the Inland Revenue or the Charity Commissioners about the meaning which should be placed on the wording of the governing instrument should be incorporated.

The end result should be a clear statement - probably quite short - which sets out what the trustees consider the governing instrument actually requires the trustees to aim for. This may be a very broad aim, or it might be a very precise purpose, depending on the exact wording of the governing instrument.

It is advisable that, at least once a year, the trustees should look at this mission statement again to remind themselves exactly of their overall remit and responsibility. It is amazing how whole areas of the purpose of the charity, as detailed in the governing instrument, can be by-passed by trustees who are busy with the one small area that they or their predecessors have marked out for action. This aspect of the life of charitable trusts is often overlooked.

The long term plan

Charities and voluntary organisations are in the business of providing service to the community - often to a particular class or group of beneficiaries - but also through them to the general public. What will be the future need for the aims set out in the mission statement? What new opportunities may present themselves in the next decade or two for the sort of service provided by the charity? Will it be for more of the same sort of charitable service, or is the demand likely to change? Is one aspect of the work going to become more and more (or less and less) needed? What threats to the survival and success of the organisation may arise? Will there still be a need for the charity in the long term future? How will things change? Is there a need for a long term strategy for the income side - for raising money - as well as for the charitable services side?

To answer these questions it will be necessary for the trustees to do some research and to engage in a lot of thinking and discussion. The less clear the picture that can be drawn of the future, the more there is a need to build in flexibility of response on the part of the organisation by preserving options in the planning.

The following example illustrates the processes involved.

Let us suppose there is a charitable trust that has been in existence for some time but there are some new trustees and they want to plan ahead. The purpose of the trust, let us suppose, is to help deprived children in the inner cities. So the first two questions the trustees have to ask is how, for the puposes of the trust, they define 'children' and how they define 'deprived'. Next they must decide what constitutes a 'city' for their purpose and how they decide which is the 'inner part' of the city.

They need to get some idea of the size of the problem - is it a thousand children or a million? They need to see what prospects there are for greater help in the future for such children - is there any possibility of the Government moving in (or further in) to help in this area? What other charities and agencies are active in this particular field? What are their plans for the future?

They will need to do some research and to gather the information they need. They next need to ask how urgent are the different aspects of the problem. They need to see where a small amount of help would have the maximum impact on the problems. In the course of all of this they will become much more knowledgeable about the whole subject and they will find that ideas take shape as to what are the long term requirements. These might include help in education, or financial help for teenagers to get jobs, or maybe holiday homes in the country for ailing children. Probably their executive officer already has an intimate knowledge of the whole business of helping deprived children, although of course they must not rely only on his view.

Out of a myriad possibilities some valid aims - which may seem almost visionary at this point - will be discerned. Much discussion will be needed by the trustees to produce an end result which should be the formulation of definite objectives which cannot possibly be achieved in a year or two, and which will need effort, planning and commitment. Such aims will almost certainly seem too ambitious and beyond their grasp. An alternative is that they decide their future policy should be to avoid all growth and to seek to preserve the status quo. Even that course may call for considerable planning.

When the research is completed and the trustees have done their thinking, have discussed and made their decisions, it will be necessary to write down in perhaps a few paragraphs the agreed long term plan. Choose a point of time about ten years ahead - sufficiently far ahead to prevent trying to plan in detail. This releases the thinking from the paralysis of working out how, in detailed terms, what is being set down as desirable and necessary can be achieved. At the same time, of course, long term objectives must be within the bounds of possibility. Once agreed, that long term plan brings everything else into focus.

The plan will set out clearly what it is thought the organisation should develop into over the next five to ten years - surviving and succeeding in a changing world. It will contain both unquantified and quantified aims. For example: '...and ten new hostels each taking fifty people, and a recognition across Britain that we are a national charity.'

Above all, the long term plan will embody what the trustees see on the horizon for their charity. More than anyone else it is they who bear the responsibility for peering into the mists of the future and deciding which direction the charity should take.

Planning for the future is hard work but it is also creative. All the trustees should be involved in the process and they will probably need plenty of time at successive meetings. They may create a working party to do some of the preliminary and detailed thinking, in which they will probably involve the executive officer as his advice and his intimate knowledge of the area in which the charity is working will be invaluable.

Once agreed, the long term plan will need to be reviewed every two or three years but, if the work has been done well it should not need much change. One reason for reviewing the plan every two or three years is to see whether any totally unforeseen and radical changes in the environment or the circumstances of the organisation have occurred. The uncertainty of the future cannot be removed by planning, but regular review can ensure that timely notice is taken of unforeseeable changes.

The medium term plan

At this point in the planning framework the vision has to be translated into a practical plan. It is at the medium term stage that definite quantified objectives are set up for achievement within a certain period of time. This part of the process is like a bridge between the long range strategy and the short term day to day jobs that will need doing. It defines what point the organisation should reach in three years time in its attempt to achieve its long term plan.

Trustees will need the input of the executive officer to help them think through what precise objectives are possible and desirable in the next three years. After discussion they may decide some further research is necessary. The trustees may wish to ask a small sub committee (or working party) to undertake specific aspects of investigation or exploration. Experts may need to be called upon to help the trustees think through the issues without blinkers. Eventually, however, the trustees, and they alone, must decide what the three year objectives of the medium term plan should be and whether they go sufficiently far towards their long term plan.

Their decision will take into account the resources of the organisation, or lack of them, including money, premises, equipment, stock, people and expertise. It is an essential part of the planning process that

Figure 20: Planning: four stages

First step			
--→			
MISSION STATEMENT			
Second step			
---→			
LONG TERM STRATEGY			
Third Step			
---→			
MEDIUM TERM PLANS			
Fourth Step			
--------------------------------------→			
SHORT TERM PLANS			
12 Months	3 Years	5 to 10 Years	Open Ended

they also take into account how they think the environment may alter in the next three years. The higher the degree of uncertainty in this, the more they will need to leave alternative courses of action available in their plans.

At the end of the process a document will be produced setting out definite quantified objectives to be achieved by the end of the third year.

Once agreed, this document will become the basis for the next stage of planning, which is carried out by the executive officer (whose contribution has already helped to shape the final result of the medium term plan). The objectives should remain in place for the whole three year period unless drastic unforeseen circumstances occur.If results in any one year depart significantly from the plan, for either better or worse, this may have an effect on the other plans already agreed for current or future years. Some fine tuning may prove necessary and this can be done annually at review time.

Early in the third year of the plan the board should start to prepare the next medium term plan.

The short term plan

Having received the medium term plan which has been agreed by the trustees, the executive officer, usually with the involvement of his staff, puts together his recommendations for the next twelve months and a plan of how these objectives should be tackled. This means assessing existing resources against requirements, deadlines and dates.

At the end of this process the executive officer produces a definite, quantified draft plan for the next twelve months which sets out the objectives for that period. If achieved, it will mean the organisation will have accomplished the first step of the three stage plan. In a further two years' time, when the next two steps are completed,the objectives of the three year medium term plan should have been accomplished.

At this stage the short term plan is still called a 'draft plan' because it is only the proposals of the executive officer and these have to be agreed finally by the trustees.

This draft short term plan (for the next twelve months) is then taken to the board meeting and discussed. The executive officer will wish to explain the reasoning behind his plan, and how its achievement will set the organisation satisfactorily on course to achieve the three year plan which has already been agreed by the board. He will also need to explain what resources are needed to implement his plan and will wish to ensure that the provision of such resources has the trustees' backing. The trustees may need to be involved in the raising of funds, or at least to agree to this being put in hand.

After the trustees have discussed, and possibly amended the short term plan, they will formally approve it and it then becomes the operational plan for the organisation for the ensuing twelve months.

After twelve months the executive officer will again present his short term plan for the following year (i.e. the second step of the three year plan) and the trustees will assess the results of the first year and decide whether the second year's plan will achieve satisfactory progress towards the objectives set by the medium term plan. The same process happens again at the beginning of the third year.

Timing of the planning function

The timing of the various stages in the planning process depends totally on the particular circumstances of the organisation. It is wise to allow at least two months or two board meetings, whichever is the longer period, for preparation of the mission statement and for the long term plan, and a further similar period for preparation of the medium term plan, with at least one to two months and one board meeting for the construction and agreement of the short term plan by the board.

Monitoring operations

At this point we come to the crux of the supervisory function of the board. Excellent plans may be agreed by the board but, unless the results are monitored by the board members, the whole exercise may well prove fruitless. Indeed, for the board to fail to monitor progress is tantamount to an abrogation of their responsibility. It should be noted that, while it is imperative that the board members have oversight of the working out of the plan, this monitoring function falls a long way short of operational management.

How does monitoring by the trustees differ from operational management which itself contains a monitoring function? It is obvious that the power and authority of the board must be delegated to the executive officer so that he can manage the operation and achieve in the agreed time frame the objectives agreed with the trustees. He has the responsibility of operational management and will himself monitor all aspects of the operation. Monitoring is an essential function in such a management role, covering all aspects of the organisation over which he has authority.

It is important that the trustees do not interfere in the management role of the executive officer. They give him authority to do a job in a certain period and they must leave him to do it. Constant interference would be intolerable and give the executive officer valid grounds for complaint. However, the trustees cannot completely ignore what is happening - that would be tantamount to letting go completely of their responsibilities. They need to know that the organisation is 'healthy', and that matters are proceeding according to plan. To do this they need to receive assurances and data that satisfies them that all is well. They must monitor periodically so that they can be content that the organisation as a whole is on course.

The trustees will have a wider vision than the executive officer, who is primarily concerned with achieving the short and medium term plans. Their horizon must extend beyond three years to the long term plan they have agreed. This means that they have a different perspective on the organisation. At the same time they are monitoring the performance of the executive officer to see that his work is satisfactory.

If some event takes place which drastically affects the long term plan of the organisation (but which appears to have no immediate effect on the short term position) they will need to sit down together with the executive officer to see whether the change should affect the plans of the current period. For example, if the Government announced plans for the future which had drastic long term effects, the trustees might need to change the three year plan accordingly, and this might have repercussions on the plan for the current year.

If we compare the board to a group of owners who own just one ship and a valuable cargo which it plans to transport across the world, it is easier to see their different perspectives. The executive officer may be likened to the captain. The owners (trustees) and the captain sit down together and agree a destination and route for the ship (and its cargo) which then sets off on its voyage. All day to day running of the ship is totally within the province of the captain (unless otherwise agreed at the outset) and he deals with day to day plans and problems, commands the crew, ensures the safety of the cargo and keeps the ship itself in good trim. The owners, however, do not just forget the ship until it reaches port again. In view of the great value of the cargo - and the ship itself - they receive regular reports of its position. If a major hurricane or some other crisis looms on the horizon they will be involved in alterations to plans. If the demand for the cargo at the destination port alters they may change both route and destination. The captain is able to consult them on any matter he wishes, and they may ask the captain for an update on various matters from time to time.

The captain is obliged to answer any questions put to him by the owners - it is their ship and their cargo and he is an employee. If the owners become too demanding or start interfering in matters which should be left to the discretion of the captain then he must endeavour to show them that they can safely leave such matters in his hands. If they continue to be a nuisance in this way his next option is to remonstrate. His final option, when all else has failed, is to resign. Clearly the parallel cannot be sustained too far, but it does illustrate certain aspects of the relationship.

How well the trustees perform their monitoring role is the true test of the effectiveness of the trustees. They must monitor through receiving information, or data, that informs them of what is actually happening and whether their plans are being fulfilled. As the trustees need a stream of data to assess whether their plans are being fulfilled, they must receive this both from the executive officer and, where financial data is concerned, from the treasurer.

Maximum effectiveness in the supervisory function of the trustees is achieved by obtaining from the executive officer and the treasurer just sufficient of the right data at the correct time to form an accurate assessment of the true state of affairs. Correcting action for one reason or another may be necessary from time to time to put the organisation back on plan. Too much data and the trustees are in danger of being swamped with too many figures; too little data and they risk being unaware that the ship is going dangerously off course.

Many boards of trustees never specify what information they require, relying instead on the judgement of the executive officer to offer them the information he thinks they need, instead of requiring him to produce what the trustees decide are the key indicators that will show whether or not the organisation is on course. Often this is because the trustees do not understand their role, do not know what to ask for, or are not sure quite when they require the information. Because of this lack of definition they are flying blind when they make decisions. In such circumstances the financial realities can become the only factor for assessing whether the trust is on course. The trustees often accept uncritically the statements by the executive officer - perhaps because they do not wish to upset him - and there is little or no real debate as to the best way forward, merely general agreement with the views expressed by the executive officer.

We are now at the heart of the difference between unsuccessful and mediocre organisations, and those that excel. A brilliant executive officer can carry inadequate trustees along for a time, but eventually their weight will drag the organisation down, whereas really good trustees can lift an ailing organisation that has a mediocre executive officer, replacing him eventually if he fails to perform. A good board of trustees with a good executive officer and working as a team will obviously achieve the best results.

There are several ways for trustees to fulfil their obligation to maintain effective oversight, that is, to obtain the information they need to monitor the trust effectively. The following checklist should help the trustees monitor effectively, without straying into the area of operational management.

1. Key indicators

Set in place a method of providing regular feedback of whatever information is necessary to check that the key stages of the plan are progressing to the satisfaction of the trustees. Some data required may be subjective, some will be in numeric form. Each year the information can be redefined until just the key indicators are called for. If trustees meet quarterly, figures can be provided in the same format for each meeting. They will probably be figures produced as at the end of the previous month. What the trustees need are the key indicators in each of the important areas of work to enable them to judge the progress and health of the organisation.

How does one decide which are the key indicators? Some of the data will be financial and may have been obtained by the treasurer; other data may relate to particular aspects of the organisation which are not financial but which seem of key importance to the trustees. Each organisation will have different needs, and these will change from time to time. Examples might be the amount of donations received each month, or the number of donations received each month, or the number of requests arriving at the charity for help of a particular sort.

2. Reports

Require the executive officer to report verbally (possibly supplemented by a written report, circulated with the agenda) at each board meeting (or at least quarterly) on progress against plans and budgets.

3. Alarm bells

Set appropriate 'alarm' bells in place. These are key indicators of real danger to the health of the organisation as distinct from key indicators of the fulfilment of the plan agreed. For example, in one organisation the number of overtime hours worked, or numbers of staff resignations in any calendar month might be crucial.

It is important to stress again that overseeing the performance of the organisation by these indicators should not trespass on the authority of the executive officer. When the trustees require this information it does not in any way detract from his job. It does not remove decision making in that area from the executive officer. He continues to have the job of managing the organisation and the trustees must let him perform that job without interfering. To fulfil their role they must keep a watching brief.

The trustees have to decide for themselves from time to time exactly how closely they need to monitor events and which key indicators they require. They will also accept the help of the executive officer when considering the matter. They may vary the information they call for as often as they see fit. Nothing should hinder them from fulfilling their obligation to be responsible for the overall health of the organisation. Naturally, they will minimise the amount of data they call for in order to reduce the time, trouble and expense they cause the administration.

Reviewing the plans

Plans may need amending for a number of reasons - for example, because of radical or unexpected changes in the environment. Changing one plan may well have repercussions on the other plans made by the trustees.

While the long term plan needs to be reviewed every two or three years, the medium term plan (which spans only three years before a new one is needed) should be reviewed annually in the light of the results of the past year; serious under or over performance could call for a change. The short term plan for the next twelve months will need to be reviewed during the current year - possibly quarterly. Each of these reviews will examine the effects of any changes in the various other plans.

Periodic review of the planning process itself

Periodically it is necessary to check on the method as well as the results of planning. When serious planning is first attempted by an organisation it has to undergo a learning process. Inevitably, mistakes are made. However, the value and importance of planning should not be dismissed simply because the first attempts produce problems.

How is it possible to get better at formulating plans?

- If decisions were made which caused problems, was the information on which they were made appropriate in the first place?

- Was the information insufficient or did it arrive too late?

- How well did the board deal with the interaction of the various plans on each other when there were changes in its short, medium or long term plans?

- Did the board call for unnecessary data or indulge in over-planning (this, however, is a rare disease!)?

- Did the planning process really enable the objectives to be achieved more efficiently?

Whatever else happens, the chairman must not let day to day crises use up the time needed by the board meeting for the planning function.

Figure 21: Elements in the review process

When attempting to assess how good the board is at planning the following questions will serve as starters:

1. Data/Information
Did we have enough before us when we decided the plan?
Was the data in sufficient detail?
Did we understand the detail sufficiently?
Was it, or the way it was presented, misleading in any way?
Could we have been better informed in any way?

2. Resources
Had we sufficient grasp of the extent of our existing resources at the time of planning?
Did we properly assess what our plans would require in resources?
Did we anticipate correctly what we would receive?
Were we too optimistic/pessimistic? Why?
Did we understand the difficulties of obtaining resources?
Did we do sufficient planning to increase our resources?
Did we listen carefully enough to the executive officer and the experts about what would be involved?

3. Staff
Did we properly assess the staff situation (numbers and competence) and foresee the problems and opportunities?
Did we assess the training needs accurately?
Did we estimate direct and indirect staff costs well? If not, why not?
Did we assess properly the difficulty or ease of obtaining replacement or new staff?

4. Monitoring/Checking
Were our processes of checking (on the safety and use of assets, and against fraud, error and waste) good enough? Were they too costly?
Were our processes of monitoring efficient?
Did we ask for the right key figures, and get them in time?
Were trustees able to ask for special figures and information from the staff from time to time - and get them when they wanted them?

5. How can we improve things for next year?

Chapter 8

Management of Employed Staff

If the trustees employ one or more people it is important that good staff policies are agreed and implemented as early as possible. Responsibility for people lays a prime obligation on the employer, and the fact that the trustees are not in day to day control of the staff who report to the executive officer must not lessen the concern of the trustees to be good employers.

It is unfortunately true that staff employed in the voluntary sector - as in the commercial sector - are sometimes underpaid, over worked, and suffer from poor management. It is not unusual to find the staff of charities provided with poor premises and equipment. Trustees without business experience sometimes do not understand the extent of their responsibilities in this area, and may be unaware of the need to find out how their staff feel about the way they are dealt with and managed.

The executive officer must be accountable in all areas to his top supervisory body which must exercise positive supervision. Nowhere is this more true than in the field of staff management. It is the responsibility of the trustees to ensure that their policy as regards staff is carried into effect but, where they employ a number of staff, they must gain this assurance despite their non-involvement in the operational management themselves. How can they do this?

The next section examines how the trustees should manage the executive officer, and then how they should relate to and deal with the staff who report to him.

The Executive Officer

1) Role

This person is the senior employee to whom all other employees report. He is by definition the head of the operational management of the organisation. It is therefore a position of considerable power. It is vital that the trustees manage him in the proper way.

He is employed by the trustees to whom he reports, but as they will normally meet only infrequently they have to depend on the executive officer for the information they need in order to perform their supervisory role. This means the executive officer is in a position of considerable power in relation to them as well.

For both those to whom the executive officer is accountable and those accountable to him, the executive officer is pivotal - probably more so than someone in a similar position in most commercial companies.

For these reasons it is doubly important for the trustees to put in place a flow of information to themselves, on a regular as well as on an *ad hoc* basis. It is no excuse for them to plead, if they are found to have failed to supervise properly, that they did not know things were going wrong. It is their responsibility to know, since they not only carry the ultimate responsibility, but also possess the power and means to obtain the essential information. If they fail to exercise these powers, important matters may pass them by; they may become so out of touch and so dependent on the executive officer that they may not even be aware that anything is wrong until the whole organisation is past recovery.

However worthy an executive officer is, the temptation to omit to report information which reflects badly on him or on the organisation, or is unwelcome for some other reason, is strong. Likewise the desire to report something in a more favourable light than is justified is constantly present. To succumb is easy. A blurring of the truth might pass undetected by the trustees unless they are aware of the need for vigilance and good oversight practices. An executive officer can easily justify his actions to himself - especially if he is able to see the problem as only a temporary one.

It is worth underlining again the basic fact on which the relationship between the trustees and the executive officer is based: he is a paid employee who reports to and is totally answerable to the trustees.

I have known cases where the executive officer has become autocratic and has acted as though the organisation belonged to him. This attitude is understandable because of the unusual concentration of power and authority that rests in his hands. The blame for a situation like this must always lie with the trustees who have allowed the situation to develop. It is they who must insist on full accountability to themselves in all areas of the life of the organisation. A weak board can easily run into problems of this sort.

Full accountability by the executive officer implies the provision of sufficient information, both regularly and on an *ad hoc* basis, to enable the trustees to monitor the health of the organisation effectively. Like doctors, they must be able to see the signs and to diagnose serious trouble when it occurs and to take emergency action if necessary. Sometimes it is useful for the trustees to call in outside help.

2) Boundaries

Under this heading comes perhaps one of the main requirements for a successful relationship between the trustees and the executive officer: the need for definition of the extent of the power and authority of the executive officer.

It is possible for a charity - especially a small charity - to operate satisfactorily for a time without the limits of power and authority being clearly defined. However, when trouble arises, as is bound to happen sooner or later in such an undefined situation, there tends to be much hurried consultation and mistakes are made in the heat of the moment. There are five areas where the executive officer needs clear direction in order to perform effectively:

Figure 22: Boundaries

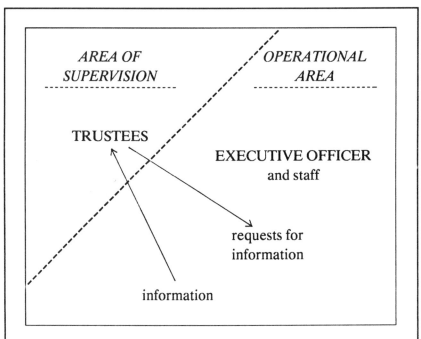

Trustees must not stray into the operational area. They have delegated authority for all of this area to the executive officer.

Their overall responsibility is for the health and progress of the whole organisation and they must obtain all the information they need to check on that health, without interfering directly in the operation area which comes under the control of the executive officer. They can, of course, instruct the executive officer on any matter they wish.

Overall control lies with the trustees.

Operational control lies with the executive officer, under the supervision of the trustees.

The boundaries of power and authority of the executive officer need definition by the trustees.

- what is expected of him (job description), and over what period it is expected (plans).

- what he can and cannot do without reference to someone else (discretionary powers).

- how he can get access to guidance and help when he is unsure of his powers or direction - new problems are bound to surface sooner or later (line of communication to the trustees).

- what information, on either a regular basis or *ad hoc* basis, he is expected to provide by when and to whom (report back).

- how and when he can have periodic personal interviews with his chairman and/or board members (personal review).

3) Job description

The executive officer needs to have a clear definition of what is expected of him, what tasks he is to undertake and what his responsibilities are. These matters should be defined at the time of his engagement and set down in a job description.

If for some reason, no job description was agreed when the executive officer was appointed, it is worth trying to rectify the omission, assuming that relations between the executive officer and the trustees are good. It can be helpful to ask the executive officer to write down a first draft of what he considers his job to be. Tactful discussions can be initiated between the trustees and the executive officer if a significant gap is revealed between their concept of the job and his.

The job description can be a difficult document to write - it is never easy to decide how much detail should be included. In view of employment legislation, as well as in the interests of getting the working relationship on a proper footing from the beginning, it is worth giving considerable attention to the formulation of the job description at the time the executive officer is recruited. The aim is to set out clearly in general terms the essential nature of the job, to specify any particular aspects which override the others in importance and to make clear the minimum requirements, specifying also the power and authority being delegated. It is often a good idea to obtain professional help with the recruitment of and job description for the executive officer.

If there are areas or activities of the organisation which are to be excluded from the remit of the executive officer, or where his power and authority are curtailed for any reason, it is necessary to state these clearly; otherwise it may be assumed they are to be included in the powers of general management. The trustees should make clear that they may from time to time alter the boundaries not only of the job, but also of his powers and authority. Without this caveat, any necessary minor redefinition of boundaries might be seen by the executive officer as a diminution of the original job.

If, for example, the trustees do not wish any staff to be dismissed without their prior agreement, this boundary condition could be either stated, or at least alluded to in the job description by an omnibus phrase such as '...subject to the directions of the trustees from time to time...' The specific direction could be made verbally to the executive officer at the time of his recruitment. What is aimed at here is the fullest understanding between the executive officer and his employers before he accepts the job. He needs to understand what he can and cannot do. He needs to accept in principle that he is totally responsible to the trustees and must not labour under any misconception that he is not fully accountable. It is also essential that he accepts their right to monitor any or all aspects without seeing it as evidence of distrust or lack of confidence. Likewise, of course, the executive officer needs to know that he is receiving sufficient power and authority (without unnecessary interference) to do the job.

Much of the job description may be written in general terms, with specific objectives and targets kept for the planning and budget documents produced from time to time.

4) Problems arising between trustees and the executive officer

(a) From the trustees' side:

(i) lack of control

If the trustees have not fully understood their role in the total organisation they will probably err on the side of exercising too little control and management. This is the normal situation because all operational power lies with the executive officer, as well as all the knowledge and information about the actual operational organisation. This tends automatically to put the executive officer in the driving seat and to call for the trustees to perform a supporting role. Often they have no real knowledge of what is actually going on in the organisation, or what the real issues are. If board meetings are few and far between, and if the trustees do not call for definite and specific data, it is likely that their involvement will in effect be limited to what the executive officer decides to tell them in a verbal report coupled with the answers to any questions they can think of on the spur of the moment, at the meeting.

Many trusts survive - for a time - on this basis, but the situation can easily and quickly deteriorate. The executive officer can become too powerful and become dismissive of the trustees - this is especially the case where the executive officer is the founder or the person with the original vision, but, because of his unique position, is not a trustee. In these circumstances, the trustees might begin to see themselves as having merely a 'rubber stamp' function and so lose interest and go.

Sometimes trustees concern themselves almost exclusively with how the finances are going, whether there are enough funds coming in, how expenses match budget, and with passing the necessary accounts.

All this is, of course, a pale shadow of their true role and the fault lies squarely at the door of the trustees. If they do not call for the data they need to really understand how the organisation is faring, and if they do not take a real grasp on the affairs of the trust, including planning, then it is almost inevitable that the executive officer will fill the vacuum by providing some information, but keeping hold of the reins of power (and information) himself. With inadequate trustees of this sort, the executive officer has to become the one who really holds the organisation together and on course.

(ii) lack of direction

Likewise, if the trustees are without any clear idea of where they wish the organisation to go - have no sense of direction - then naturally they can be of little assistance to the executive officer. He needs to have goals, be properly accountable to the board and be called upon to give full account of his work periodically.

(iii) unwillingness to make decisions or take risks

Sometimes trustees have been ineffective for so long that they have become lazy and do not wish to be disturbed from an easygoing attitude. A crisis may pull them together but sometimes it is too late. They may be indecisive and unwilling to do the hard thinking that is necessary to analyse some of the problems. If they have an incorrect concept of what being a trustee involves, they may be quite unprepared to face hard questions or potential risks that need assessment and decision. If they are badly led by their chairman they may never properly understand what is required of them in a well run trust.

(iv) irresponsibility

It is also possible for trustees to be irresponsible in various ways. They may make decisions without due care for the consequences, perhaps forcing those decisions on the executive officer. Their irresponsibility may extend to lack of integrity, in which case they may take short cuts that take them perilously near the precipice edge.

It is also irresposible to act within the operational area without the agreement of the executive officer, unless they are so acting because they have decided to overrule his authority and power for some very important reason. They would be justified in doing this if the safety of the assets of the trust were being put seriously at risk if they did nothing.

It is easy act irresponsibly by trespassing in the territory of the executive officer. If the boundaries of the powers delegated to the executive officer have not been laid down clearly, or if the board members have little business experience, it is only too easy for one of them to make matters very difficult for the executive officer. For example, a trustee may visit the premises of the organisation unannounced and wander around talking to the employed (or volunteer) staff and listening sympathetically to unreal grievances, thereby undercutting the authority of the executive officer.

A good chairman will ensure that all his board members are fully alive to the dangers that could result from such actions. He will insist that the territory of the executive officer (the operational area) is respected. The executive officer is in complete charge in the operational area, and board members have no right to interfere or to cause trouble. Normally, they will be invited in by the executive officer, or at least go in with his agreement. After such a visit they should tell the executive officer immediately of any problems of which they have become aware on their visit. They should not on any account interfere in the authority and direction of the executive officer or cast any doubt on his decisions, views or attitudes. They need to be particularly careful in conversations with staff who report to the executive officer.

The opposite fault can also arise: trustees can be so uninterested in the organisation that they never go near the premises or meet the staff. This form of irresponsibility may become a demotivating factor for the staff - and it might lessen the respect of the staff for their own executive officer who, they imagine, does not have the full support of the board members.

Great sensitivity is needed by board members to ensure they do not cause problems by encroaching on the territory of the executive officer.

(v) lack of contact with the executive officer

There can also be a vacuum in the relationships between the board members and the executive officer. They may only meet in the course of board meetings several times a year, and have no other contact. This may lead the executive officer to feel isolated and alone in his task of heading the organisation.

(b) From the executive officer's side.

(i) a defensive attitude

It is possible for the executive officer to cause problems for the board members by his attitude. He may be so firmly in charge of 'his' organisation that he sees any incursion from a member of the board as a possible threat, in which case he will tend to warn the trustees off 'his territory' as much as he can. He may be loath to let any board member wander freely about the organisation's offices, without being in attendance himself. He may call for lengthy notice before he arranges such a visit. He may try to keep the board members away from some areas of the organisation or away from meeting some or all of the staff.

It is easy for board members, faced by such an unwelcoming attitude, to be discouraged. They may cease to bother trying to show interest by visits to the premises when, clearly, they are not welcome.

(ii) monopolising information

An executive officer can cause problems by failing to supply the board with enough of the right information, or by supplying it at the meeting itself in so much detail that it cannot be assimilated in the time available. It is not suggested that in all such cases deceit or dishonesty is necessarily intended. It may simply be an attitude adopted by an executive officer without his realising that, although he knows everything about the running of the organisation, trustees may have problems mastering even the basic facts. Such an attitude on the part of the executive officer may discourage the board members from making the effort to obtain the information they need about the organisation.

Normally, of course, there is no need for the trustees to know a great deal of detail, but they do need enough to be satisfied that they understand thoroughly what is going on *(see page 101)* and whether their plans are working out.

If the executive officer does not supply details to board meetings in an open, organised and detailed way, the trustees are left with whatever crumbs of information they can pick up at board meetings or by hearsay. It is up to them to call for whatever information they need, or think they may need. They must ask for specific information to be supplied on a regular basis if necessary.

(iii) poor motivation

The executive officer may be poorly motivated - and one of the causes of this might be unreasonable trustees! His low motivation can cause problems in his relationship with the board. He may have personal problems at home, he may have been blocked by the trustees from what he had set his heart on doing, or he may have lost interest in the aims of the charity. He may have lost the vision with which he set out, or be already thinking of what job he is going to move to in the near future. There may be any of a thousand reasons.

(iv) employee problems

If the executive officer has unsatisfactory relationships with the paid and/or volunteer staff under him, this may lead to problems in his relationship with the board. He may draw back from formulating plans until he is more sure of staff support, but not wish to divulge the reason for his lack of enthusiasm to the trustees. He may wish to hide the fact that there is incipient revolution. In any case he will probably desire to preserve his own reputation and position.

5) Periodic interviews of the executive officer

Once in place the executive officer rapidly becomes the pivotal person in the organisation. To the staff and to the trustees - as well as to the beneficiaries and the general public - he becomes the person in top executive authority. Because he is such a key person, there should be a formal interview at least once a year - probably conducted by two trustees, one of whom may be the chairman.

This formal interview should take place despite the frequent contact between executive officer and trustees. Normally it is the board chairman who sees most of the executive officer and he should be sufficiently close to the situation to know if there is a problem, and to diagnose the cause. A wise chairman will be able to create a good relationship with the executive officer and often he will become guide, philosopher and friend as well as employer.

6) Interviews with a prospective executive officer

The trustees will wish to assess the motivation of a prospective executive officer throughout the interview. They will wish to be sure that he is fully in sympathy with the aims of the organisation, has the necessary experience and is the sort of person they can work with in the context of the board meeting. There are various subjects that trustees might wish to discuss with a prospective executive officer at the initial interviews:

1. The trustees will wish to give an assessment of the point reached in the development of the work of the charity and, in general terms, where they want the charity to go. Do they expect slow, moderate or rapid growth - or no growth at all? Do they anticipate an increase in the number of staff? What is their vision for the work?

2. The trustees will wish to confirm to the executive officer that, while the strategic and medium term planning is firmly in the province

of the board of trustees (albeit, with the help of the executive officer), they will expect the executive officer to produce detailed annual plans in conformity with the longer term plans, and to operate a budgeting system. The timetable should be explained so that the executive officer realises that he will need to produce annually both clearly defined specific plans and budgets for approval by a board meeting.

3. The trustees will look for agreement by the executive officer that specific information, supplied both periodically and *ad hoc*, will be required at board meetings. In addition, the trustees will expect him to provide the trustees with a full update and details of any matter about which he considers they might wish to know.

4. Apart from the general management of the organisation and close liaison with the trustees, the executive officer may need to be responsible for raising funds along the lines of policy agreed by the board. What is expected by the trustees must be explored thoroughly and be accepted by the executive officer.

5. What are the boundary conditions *(see page 111)* and will the executive officer be allowed to change the way things are done in the organisation? What scope will be allowed for innovation? Will he receive the resources he needs for an acceptable suggestion? Do the trustees accept that he needs a free rein to run the organisation his way, provided he keeps to the policy and general guidelines of the trustees?

6. Will the executive officer be expected to work entirely on his own between board meetings? Would he prefer it that way or would he prefer close liaison with the chairman or with some other trustee who can speak for the board?

7. Can the executive officer hire and fire staff without prior reference to the trustees, provided he is working within guidelines laid

down by them? Can he determine salary scales? Is the approach of the trustees similar to that of the executive officer?

8. To whom does the executive officer refer as regards his own situation? Will he have an formal set interview once a year with the chairman or someone else to check on his own situation and aspirations?

9. Is the executive officer willing to accept that the trustees will change their requirements from time to time and may call for more or less information, and that this should not be taken as any reflection on him? Does he accept the right of the trustees to radically change the direction of the charity in the unlikely event that they come to think they need such a change?

Staff reporting to the executive officer

If more than one member of staff is employed, the executive officer will be in the relationship of a manager to them. While he must have authority and power to manage them fully this does not absolve the board from responsibility for ensuring that good staff relations and good staff policies and practices are in place and are being observed.

Such matters as pay, remuneration package, conditions, overtime, holidays, interviewing, and so forth, obviously all come under the responsibility of the executive officer as operational matters, but trustees need to be assured that a satisfactory policy is in force. How they do this depends on the circumstances but normally the executive officer would report on all staff matters once a year, with a review of the staff position.

Clear policy should be laid down by the board as regards how far they wish to be involved in taking on and dismissing staff who report to the executive officer.

It is essential that the trustees recognise the authority of the executive officer over the other employed staff. They must not trespass on his territory by dealing directly with the staff in the wrong way. They have delegated to the executive officer the control of staff, and they must not cause him difficulty in this area.

The trustees may wish to lay down a recognised procedure for a member of the staff to appeal to them following a decision on certain specified matters by the executive officer, or even generally. If so, the procedure should be laid down in writing and all staff should made aware of it.

A particular problem can arise because the treasurer may need to have a close liaison with and, indeed, to give instructions to, the full time member(s) of staff in charge of financial matters - whom we will refer to as the finance officer *(see page 73)*. This person reports to the executive officer, not to the treasurer. The finance officer must refer any problems arising from his working for two masters (treasurer and executive officer) to the executive officer.

If the treasurer meets difficulties on any important financial matter - for example, in obtaining financial information he requires - he should discuss it first with the executive officer. If that course fails to produce the desired result, he should probably then refer it to the chairman and the next meeting of the board of trustees. Obviously how this is done will depend on the circumstances of the particular organisation.

The management of volunteers

In addition to the trustees, who perform their duties in a voluntary capacity, many charities recruit volunteers to help in fundraising or administration or to assist in the work of the charity in some other way. Such voluntary help normally comes under the control and management of the executive officer, where one is appointed.

Trustees have the overall responsibility for all aspects of the charity and they will wish to assure themselves that the policy regarding volunteers is a good one and that the executive officer is maintaining effective management over their work. What are the main elements of policy and practice for which they need to look?

The greatest need is for a businesslike approach to the whole matter. This is the best way to make the experience rich and rewarding for the person giving their time and effort, and for the charity to gain most from what is so generously given.

It is advisable in all cases, except possibly where the help given is purely casual and occasional, to have an application form completed as if the volunteer were applying for paid employment. The degree of detail on the form depends on needs of the charity and the work the volunteer will be doing. From this document the staff of the charity can make an initial assessment and decide whether to go forward to an interview.

The next stage is for the prospective voluntary worker to be interviewed. At the interview the precise nature of the job can be explained, the suitability of the person applying can be probed and any questions asked by either side. It is important for the interviewer to outline clearly the background of the charity, its aims and plans and what methods it uses. The nature of the relationship between volunteer and staff needs to be explained clearly. Guidelines of conduct and reporting should be gone through and, preferably, confirmed in some written explanatory booklet or paper.

In most cases the volunteer should be asked to provide proper references - certainly where they are handling money or when they are expected to work with vulnerable people such as the elderly or the very young.

Appointment should be a for a set period - often one year - it being understood from the outset by both sides that a review will then take place with possible reappointment for a further period, if so desired by the volunteer who should realise that the quality of their work as well as the quantity of their input is of concern to the charity and that their contribution will come under regular review.

Once accepted the voluntary worker will need training and regular briefing. They will probably need to visit the premises of the charity to see how it functions and meet some of the staff. They might also meet other volunteers who can give them valuable pointers in their forthcoming work.

In the course of their first year with the charity they should have one or more interim interviews with staff so that they can voice any problems they have, clear up any misunderstandings, obtain any help or advice and ask for any training they consider they need. Staff can encourage and, themselves, gain valuable insight into what is happening in the area where the volunteer is working.

The trustees need to be fully aware of the position regarding volunteers working for the charity and to be ready to meet some or all of them, depending on the particular circumstances. It may be that volunteers are invited to an open day once a year at which trustees are available to meet and talk with them - and to thank them.

It must be emphasised that the trustees, as employers, need to be satisfied that proper working arrangements (including insurance) have been made for voluntary staff for whom the regulations of the Health and Safety at Work apply as for fulltime staff.

Chapter 9

Managing Fundraising and Public Relations

The trustees' management of fund raising operations

What are the responsibilities of the board as a top supervisory body as regards managing the process of fundraising?

1) Responsibility of trustees

The trustees cannot dismiss fund raising as just another activity of the trust. The money raised in this way will probably be the life blood of the organisation, on which future plans and success depend. It is therefore often of the greatest importance to trustees; it is not something they can delegate and forget about for twelve months, receiving only an annual report. How the funds are raised, the public image projected by the means adopted for the raising of the funds and whether the target is reached are all of vital importance to the trust and therefore to the trustees.

Having accepted that the trustees have a prime responsibility as regards the raising as well as the spending of funds, does this mean they have themselves to become involved in the activity required actually to raise the funds?

Although it is generally accepted that the more senior the person making the approach for a sizeable donation, the more likely the donor is to give, it is true that the trustees do not necessarily have to become personally involved in fundraising. In small or medium sized charities the trustees may have to accept that they must get involved, especially if there is no one else available or competent to do the job. In larger charities however the activity has to be on a more professional basis and usually the task is delegated to the fulltime staff. The trustees retain the overall responsibility for policy and planning for fundraising even though they do not get involved in the day to day process.

One well tried way for trustees to deal with fundraising is for them to create a small fundraising sub-committee. One or two trustees, with power to co-opt several other well placed people, form a small committee with a remit to raise funds. Sometimes the treasurer is at the centre of this activity, but that is not essential. The treasurer may or may not be willing or able to become the prime mover in this area.

2) The need for detailed plans

Whether funds are to be raised by a small fundraising sub-committee, or by the executive officer and his staff, or by the whole group of trustees, a plan is essential. Realistic targets need to be set, representing a reasonable figure (sufficient for the perceived need) capable of being raised (hopefully) in a reasonable period.

It is not always recognised that it is as easy to have too small a target as it is to have too large a figure. If a charity is new and small, and has modest plans, obviously it would be quite inappropriate to fix a target of £1 million, but equally, to aim at £40,000 might be to underestimate grossly the potential. Expertise in all aspects of fundraising, especially the initial analysis, allows a charity to assess a realistic target and the prospective categories of donor by type and amount.

It is wise to explore extensively before deciding on a strategy. Apart from information derived from seminars and books, it is also possible to employ professional advisers who will help to get the thinking and planning straight. Professional fundraisers can be engaged who will assist in identifying the strategy, methods and costs and then take over the job of raising the money. *(See page 128)*

3) The need for good documentation

Most charities raise money by launching an appeal through the issue of a brochure. This document goes by various names but it is often called *The Case for Support*.

It is worth devoting considerable time and thought to *The Case for Support*. It will be the shop window; indeed, it represents the charity to most of the people who will see it, as they may not otherwise know of it at all. It has an influence on the attitude of the public generally and of donors in particular. Two or more types of brochure may be produced for the same charity, aimed at different markets.

Professional help in composing *The Case for Support* is often useful if the staff of the charity have no expertise in this area. Too glossy a production can cause donors to think the charity is extravagent, whereas a brief text can leave them with too many questions. Too factual a brochure can leave them unpersuaded and too persuasive a brochure can raise resistance against the 'sales pitch'. Getting it just right is crucial.

4) The use of professional fundraisers

Arguments run strongly both for and against professional fundraisers who, for a fee (or sometime for a percentage of the amount raised) will assume responsibility for mounting and running the campaign for funds.

Firstly, there is what might be called the ethical argument. The donors give their money for the cause: is it right that a sizeable amount will be diverted for the fee of the fundraisers?

Another argument sometimes suggested for not using professional fundraisers is that there is a need for careful negotiation and control by the trustees, otherwise they might find their charity landed with an image they much regret, or even become saddled with unacceptable financial liability (e.g. a fee plus expenses payable without results). If the trustees are aware of these dangers and proceed carefully, this argument no longer applies.

In their favour, however, is the fact that good firms do have expertise and experience in the field. They also have the drive, the ability to plan and the means to go to the right people. Many who use them are satisfied with their work. The trustees need to decide their policy, do their preliminary research into possible firms to use, discuss the matter at length and then make their own decision.

Role of trustees in public relations

In all charities, and especially in the larger ones, it is advisable for the board of trustees to decide a policy as to how they will deal with public relations. The sort of questions they will wish to consider will include:

1. Do we wish to have a high, medium or low public profile? (it may be useful to be well known publicly - for example if donations are requested from the general public).

2. What image do we wish to present to the public?

3. What are the specific objectives in this area for the next three years, and for the next twelve months?

4. How much money are we prepared to spend on achieving these objectives?

5. Who is to be responsible for preparing a budget and for implementing the policy and plans agreed, and who is to authorise expenditure of money?

6. Do we need professional help? For exactly what purpose do we need such help and how much are we prepared to spend on obtaining it? Is such help needed urgently - for example, if there is an urgent need to raise money?

7. To whom should media enquiries be directed, and what is the limit of their authority? (for example, 'the executive officer to deal with the press but all television enquiries to be referred immediately to the chairman').

8. What general policies should be laid down for statements to the media? This can be a very sensitive area for some charities.

Chapter 10

Tests For Effectiveness

The following questions are designed to build up a picture of the organisation in order to see how the board may become more effective.

Look for an assurance that proper controls and adequate monitoring mechanisms are in place in each area of importance in the organisation.

Board administration

1. Is proper notice given of meetings?

2. Are agendas and papers circulated in good time before the meeting?

3. Are minutes well done, average or poor?

4. When are minutes circulated?

5. Are all Reports and Returns submitted on time?

6. Does the executive officer report to the board verbally and/or in writing?

7. How often does the executive officer report?

8. How long do board meetings last?

9. How often does the board meet?

10. Where and when does the board meet?

11. Is it recognised that some board members have a hidden agenda (i.e. an axe to grind)?

12. Does the board allocate specific subjects to particular meetings in the year?

Board members

1. Do board members get on well together?

   - do they make a harmonious well-balanced team?
   - how are strong differences of view settled?
   - do they usually work by consensus or by vote?
   - if by consensus, should they vote more often?
   - if by vote, is it because there is little consensus?

2. Are their skills/experience complementary?

   - are there some useful skills missing?
   - what are they doing about these missing skills?

3. Is attendance good?

   - which trustees are absent most often?
   - do they spend enough time together?
   - work out overall attendance per year for the last three years and express as a percentage.

4. How much pre-meeting reading is required?

   - how much do the trustees say they actually read before the meeting?

5. How long have existing members served?.

- is there a set period for which trustees are expected to serve?
- are there new trustees coming in?

6. How is the chairman elected?

- is his election a real exercise or a foregone conclusion?
- when was the last change?
- is it clear who his successor is?

7. How does the chairman perform?

- does he command respect?
- is he autocratic?
- is his relationship with the executive officer good?
- does he bully, persuade or ignore?
- is he regarded by his fellow trustees as a manipulator?
- is he efficient in getting decisions?
- is he fair?
- does he move the business along in a meeting?

Planning

1. Is there any planning - of whatever sort?

2. Is the plan written down clearly anywhere?

- are there long, medium and/or short term plans?

3. Are the plans known by all who need to know?

4. Is progress thereon monitored by the executive officer?

5. Is progress thereon monitored by the the board?

- how often?

6. Are results reviewed annually?

    - by the executive officer with his staff?

    - by the board against targets/budgets?

7. Are objectives ever amended?

    - by the executive officer (in the light of new factors)?

    - by the board?

8. Are plans and results linked in any way to rewards of staff?

Financial matters

1. Do all board members get involved in discussions involving money?

    - if not, which do?

2. Can board members request extra information between meetings?

    - do they?

3. Are there budgets and who produces them?

    - are they understood by all board members?

    - are they really vetted by the board?

4. Are there entrenched opposing positions and a sense of battle?

    - between whom and over what?

5. Is progress monitored regularly by the treasurer?

6. Are plans adjusted in the light of progress mid-term?

7. Is the effectiveness of the budget/planning process reviewed annually?

    - in the light of results in order to improve effectiveness?

Executive Officer

1. Does he report regularly to the board on all matters?

   - nature of report: oral, written, detailed, outline only?

2. Does he take the board into his confidence?

3. Are the boundaries of his authority clearly laid down?

   - how does he observe them?

4. Does he have the confidence of the staff?

5. Does he have the right degree of initiative?

6. Does he conduct annual interviews, at least with his senior staff?

7. Do board members sometimes meet without the executive officer?

8. Does the executive officer lead or follow the board?

9. Does the executive officer get on well with the chairman/ treasurer?

10. Do the executive officer and chairman meet between board meetings?

    - how often and why?

11. Is the executive officer cost conscious?

    - does the executive officer report on costs?

    - are explanations requested and supplied at board meetings:
      about specific costs?
      about administration expenses generally?

12. Does a trustee(s) or the chairman interview the executive officer annually?

Public relations

1. Is anyone deputed to deal with public relations?

   - what in practice happens?
   - is it done well?
   - Who refers to whom when urgent problems arise?

2. Has the board considered what authority it might delegate in such matters?

3. Has a clear policy been decided by the board?

   - is there a budget?

Levels of remuneration

1. Is the remuneration package for the executive officer at the right level?

2. Is there a scale for the other staff?

   - does the scale generally seem right?

4. Are salaries and benefits reviewed annually?

   - is review linked to a realistic assessment of performance at all levels?
   - are pay and performance linked?

5. Is there a proper policy?

Chapter 11

Problem Analysis

Some of the problems that can face charities

Problem	Symptoms	Suggestions
AN INADEQUATE BOARD		
(Applies in many charities, especially if there is little or no business expertise.)	Few creative ideas Inadequate planning Poor direction	A dynamic new chairman New trustees
AN INADEQUATE CHAIRMAN		
(Applies in many charities, especially the small and medium-sized.)	Long meetings Overcrowded agendas Inadequate planning Arguments and factions on the board Fudged minutes	Change chairman Use more sub-committees

Problem	Symptoms	Suggestions
AN INADEQUATE EXECUTIVE OFFICER		
	Poor staff management	Remotivate executive officer
	Lack of drive	Give training
	Poor results	Set specific targets
		Review reporting procedures
BAD RELATIONS BETWEEN BOARD AND EXECUTIVE OFFICER		
(There are many disheartened and discouraged executive officers.)	Tense relationships on the board	Change chairman and/ or executive officer
	Over-emphasis on the minutes	Find excuse for a new start in some way
	Over strict guide- lines on executive officer	Ask executive officer to do a paper on next five years
MISGUIDED FUND RAISING		
(Without expertise themselves, the trustees think that raising money is simply a matter of effort. Early mistakes can ruin their chances of really good returns.)	Failed targets in fund raising	Call in expert
		Form sub-committee including some business people

Problem	Symptoms	Suggestions

STAFF REMUNERATION

(Often a disaster area! Trustees not infrequently expect to get their work done on the cheap. Or they are so afraid of funds drying up that they become miserly and inflict poor working conditions, and pay, on their staff.)

Discontented staff
Uninterested staff
Excessive staff
  sickness
Clock watching by
  the staff

New salary scales
Interviews by trustees
More interest in staff
  by trustees

LACK OF DIRECTION

(Without serious thought and effort there can be no real sense of direc- tion and momentum. This affects employed staff and the whole enterprise can sink into apathy.)

Preservation of the
  status quo
Inadequate planning
Weak chairman
Too many sleepy
  long term board
  members
Lack of creativity

New dynamic
  chairman
Commission sub-
  committee to study
  problem

Problem	Symptoms	Suggestions

NO DRIVE FOR EXCELLENCE

(A setting of standards and a drive for excellence throughout the organisation must stem from the trustees. If they compromise or are not motivated it is probable that others will be the same. With this there needs to be a sense of real service to whoever is being served by the organisation and society generally. This spirit should imbue the whole organisation from trustee to tea-lady.)	Sloppiness at all levels Over concentration on fund raising	Board to give urgent priority New standards from chairman downwards Trustees to take more personal interest in all areas of the organisation

Chapter 12

What Next?

The following issues might be useful as a starting point in the task of reassessing the health of your organisation.

- Check your own governing instrument. What is your 'mission'? Are you tackling yet all the aims for which you were originally set up? Are there plans to start work on those still outstanding?

- Assess the quality and performance of your trustees. Is there anything you can do now which will help in the long term? What is the balance of your board of trustees like? Does it need certain expertise which is missing at present? Does the chairman hold several names in reserve for the time when existing trustees drop out for one reason or another?

- Get a crystal clear idea of what you are aiming at - in terms that enable you to know when you have reached your objectives. Plan to have well-researched, thoroughly deliberated and agreed definite long, medium and short term plans in place.

- Pay particular attention to having satisfactory minutes. Make sure they are circulated within a few days of the meeting and mark them with who does what next.

- Ensure that the relationship between board and executive officer is good and that you (as trustee) and he are of one mind. Have you put the necessary checks in place to monitor his performance as well as the performance of the organisation?

- If the chairman is the wrong person then you probably have, or will have, great problems! Is there anything at all that can be done about it? Do you have a limitation on how long a chairman can serve?

- Make sure your treasurer is on top of all financial aspects. Is he also providing clear explanations and guidance to all the board members? Is control and best use of cash and other assets top priority?

- Are you actually checking the effectiveness of the board at least once a year on a formal basis? How can you improve your performance as a board?

- Do you need someone to come in from outside with the benefit of objectivity? He can perhaps say the things that need saying but that no-one wishes to voice for fear of conflict or of hurting someone.

- Is the note of genuine service to others paramount in the thinking of the board, and is a striving for excellence evident in all from the chairman down?

Glossary

Agenda The list of items which, it is hoped, will be dealt with at a meeting. It is usually sent out to members beforehand so that they know what they are going to be discussing. Any member can submit items for discussion by asking for them to be included on the agenda

An agenda is often referred to as a draft until it is agreed, or altered and agreed, at the beginning of the next meeting of the organisation.

Association/Society These terms refer to voluntary organisations which are not necessarily charitable. A netball club is an association, but may not be charitable.

Beneficiaries Those who benefit from the activities of a charity

Board The board of trustees.

Budgets Estimates of income or expenditure or of some other resource (for example - staff) which chart what is hoped will happen over a future period.

Charitable Trust A trust which has been constituted for charitable purposes.

Charitable Trustee A trustee of a charity, as distinct from a trustee of a private trust.

Charity No clear legal definition is available. However, it may be loosely defined as a trust or undertaking established for charitable purposes only according to the law of England and subject to the jurisdiction of the High Court. Please see page 33.

Charity Commissioners The Charity Commissioners are appointed under the Charities Act of 1960 principally to further the work of charities by giving advice and information and by investigating and checking abuses. They also make Schemes and Orders to modernise the purposes and administrative machinery of charities and to confer on trustees additional powers, give consent to land transactions by charities and maintain a register of charities. Their services to charities are free.

Committee A small group which is authorised by the main group and charged with a particular remit or function.

Constitution This is the name given to the foundation document of an organisation. It refers to the way it is structured and usually outlines in some detail how it will work. All major matters are covered: the objectives of the organisation, the type and number of officers, how they are elected, how often the members will be called together, etc.

Council of Reference Generally this is the name given to a group, which might be small or large, of named people to whom the charity looks for advice and guidance periodically. Their function is to be updated from time to time and to be consulted for their opinion and influence. Such a group often contains some prestigious people, whose names are known to those dealing with or being asked to donate to the charity. Their status helps validate the standing and worth of the charity.

Employed Staff This term is used of staff employed full or part time. It does not refer to those (such as trustees) who receive only expenses. All employed staff are assumed to be responsible to the executive officer.

Executive Committe The committee set up and authorised by trustees to deal in the interval between their meetings with whatever matters require their attention.

Executive Officer This refers to the most senior of the employed staff, although he may go by many names including chief executive officer, general secretary, clerk, and director. He heads the work of the organisation and is responsible to the top supervisory body.

Fiduciary This is a word with a legal connotation. It basically refers to some element of trust being involved. Whenever anyone acts as trustee they are bound to have regard to that trust above their own interest, and must not be influenced by or have regard to their own interests or advantage.

Governing Instrument (or document) The document which constitutes or founds an organisation. For a trust it is the trust deed. For a cricket club or other association, it may be the Rules and Regulations. It might be a Royal Charter.

Key Indicators Information - often but not always financial - that indicates the state of affairs in a particular area and which usually-has a wider significance to those monitoring the situation.

Long Term Plan The aims of the organisation for the period from 5 to 10 years hence; sometimes the period is even longer. Also referred to as the long term strategy.

Medium Term Plan The aims of the organisation for three to five years hence.

Minutes This is the name given to the record taken at a meeting and put as soon as possible into written form, circulated to members, and agreed at the next meeting as a true and accurate record of what happened and was decided. Writing minutes is a job that can be tackled by anyone - producing good minutes however requires hard work and good note keeping, plus the sense to write up the draft record within hours, not days or weeks, of the meeting.

Mission Statement A document, composed by the board of trustees, which extracts from the governing instrument (for example, the trust deed) the essence of the purpose of the trust. It sets down in clear language, with whatever explanations may be desirable, what the trust is empowered and directed to do, in the widest terms.

Non-profit making This term is used of organisations such as charities to indicate that they are not primarily commercially oriented. Such organisations may conduct business (for example, selling goods or services) but the motivation is philanthropic rather than the benefit of shareholders, members or lenders.

Patrons These are usually well known people who agree to have their name associated with the charity. Often the names of Patrons form part of the letterhead of the charity. They are not trustees and do not take part in the running of the charity.

Prima Facie This is used of evidence, and means that 'on the face of it' the evidence is to be taken as acceptable. That does not mean such evidence cannot be challenged, but that, unless it is challenged, it will be taken as agreed.

Report and Accounts These are the documents that have to be published annually by such organisations as companies. Charities are also required to produce them, with copies going to the Charity Commission and the Inland Revenue.

Resources An omnibus term, taken as applying to all types of resource - money, buildings, equipment, staff, stocks and shares, etc. Time itself might be regarded as a resource - in the nature of a wasting asset.

Royal Charter This is the formal document by which a Sovereign incorporates a body, whether it be an institute, college or some other body. It will detail its purpose and rights. When a body is so established, and is registered as a charity, it is in a different class from that of, say, a company limited by guarantee. Some of these bodies are very ancient.

Rules and Regulations These are the formal principles and organisational procedures of an organisation which are laid down at inception. Often they are only altered by a resolution in general meeting - that is, where all the members can express an opinion and vote.

Scheme of the Commissioners Where, for example, the purpose for which a charity was formed has become extinct (e.g. the need has disappeared) the trustees can apply to the Charity Commissioners who will examine the position and may then agree a Scheme for the future of the the charity with fresh aims and objectives.

Secretary The person responsible for filing official documents, organising the administration connected with board meetings and taking and filing minutes. The term is used of the person who, possibly for only one meeting, records the business of the meeting and produces the draft minutes for the chairman.

Short Term Plan The plans for the ensuing twelve months. This might be prepared and discussed several months before the commencement of the twelve month period.

Sub-Committee Usually refers to a smaller group than a committee. Itc is set up to avoid the time of a main committee being wasted on too much detail. Sometimes they continue indefinitely, sometimes they are set up for a particular purpose or period and expire thereafter.

Top Supervisory Body The most senior body of the organisation. It bears the ultimate power to make decisions, and is not responsible to any other person or group in the organisation. In a trust this would be the group of trustees, called in this handbook 'the board'. There may be some element of accountability - for example to the Charity Commissioners.

Trust Deed This is a deed, legally signed and witnessed, which sets out the constitution of the trust. It will give the names of the first trustees, state aims and objects of the trust, and so on. It may lay down who shall be chairman and for how long, the number constituting a quorum and many other details.

Trustee A person who takes on responsibility for executing the trusts laid down in the trust. See also *charitable trustee*; in this book the term is used interchangeably with charitable trustee.

Voluntary Body This term is used of any organisation which is directed by unpaid people (who may, however, receive expenses), whether or not it employs volunteers. It can include any body which has a form of organisation (although it may or may not have a written constitution). The term is taken as including charities, but goes beyond that term to include associations and non-charitable organisations

Volunteer Staff Those who give time under the direction of the board (probably through the executive officer) to help the organisation. The essential condition is that they are not paid and obtain no material benefit except expenses.

Bibliography

Covenants
Michael Norton.
Directory of Social Change
This is a practical guide to the tax advantages of giving.

Law of Trusts
L. B. Curzon
M. and E. Handbook Series
A useful and inexpensive book on the legal position.

Guidelines for Directors
The Institute of Directors

Directors Responsibilities
Cork Gully
A guide, by the insolvency division of Coopers Lybrand, to the implications of the 1986 insolvency legislation.

Law Relating to Charities
D. G. Cracknell
Oyez
This is a full and weighty legal tome.

Accounting and Financial Management for Charities
Directory of Social Change

Charities and Voluntary Organisations - The Voluntary Treasurer
Lawrence S. Fenton
Institute of Chartered Accountants for England and Wales

Meetings
L. Hall
M. and E. Handbook Series

The Fundraising Handbook
Redmond Mullin
Mowbrays

Useful Addresses

The Charities Aid Foundation
48 Pembury Road
Tonbridge
Kent TN9 2JD
Telephone (0732) 356323
Publish a Directory which is the main source book for information about grant giving trusts. This will be available for reference in your local library. They also produce other useful publication, including a magazine called 'Charity'.

The Charities Commissioners for England and Wales
St. Albans House
57-60 Haymarket
London SW1Y 4QX
Telephone: (01) 210 3000
Publish a range of booklets free of charge. Full information on request.

The Association of Charity Officers
2nd Floor, Tavistock House North
Tavistock Square
London WC1H 9RJ
It may be worthwhile contacting this association.

The Legislation-Monitoring Service for Charities
7 Market Street
Woodstock
Oxford OX7 1SU
Telephone (0993) 811357
Director: Harry Kidd

The National Council for Voluntary Organisations
26 Bedford Square
London WC1B 3HU
Telephone: (01) 636 4066
This is the umbrella body for the voluntary sector. It provides management, information and advisory services.

Index

of related interest

First-Time Publishing: How to Print and Publish your own Report
Betzy Dinesen
1990 ISBN 1 85302 047 8

More and more organisations need to issue professional, well-produced reports, bulletins and product literature, with little or no experience of the print and publishing processes. This practical handbook covers everything the small to medium-sized company, club or society, small charity or simply the novice tackling a print job will need to know, from budgeting to distributing the finished article.

The contents include: The budget. Options for different budgets. Typesetting. Using camera ready copy from word-processed output. Print runs. Printing covers and comb-binding. What the printing process is. Typesetters and printers. Types of binding. Finding a supplier. Getting and estimate. Preparing the Text. What copy editing is. What the non-professional copy editor should do. Rewriting. Dealing with technical material and tables. Late copy. Copyright. Using a professional copy editor. The role of the graphic designer. Do you need a designer? What a designer does that you can't. The visual. Proofs. Artwork and how to check it. Illustrations. Line and half- tones. Preparing diagrams and charts yourself. Using computer output. Use of colour. Half-tones: what the printer needs, cropping, using colour photographs as half-tones. Photo libraries and other sources of pictures. Making line illustrations out of photographs. Writing captions. Typesetting and proofs. Typesetting from a manuscript. Typesetting from disk. How to read proofs. Galleys. Page proofs. Colour printing. Going for a second colour. Costs. Use. Desktop publishing. Investing in a DTP system. Using a DTP bureau. Printing from a DTP, using DTP output as camera-ready copy. Learning how to use a DTP. Printing. What the printer does. Do you need printer's proofs? Deliver. Storing film for a reprint. Distribution. To clients, your company, club members. Mailing lists. Bookshops and libraries. Is your publication something for a commercial publisher? Sponsored and vanity publishing. Glossary.